LA PAELLA

DELICIOUSLY AUTHENTIC RICE DISHES FROM SPAIN'S MEDITERRANEAN COAST

LA PAELLA

Text and photographs by Jeff Koehler
Recipe photographs by Pep Blancafort

CHRONICLE BOOKS
SAN FRANCISCO

Library of Congress Cataloging-in-Publication Data available.

ISBN-10: 0-8118-5251-2
ISBN-13: 978-0-8118-5251-7

Manufactured in China.

Designed and typeset by Benjamin Shaykin
Typeset in STF Walbaum, PTF Bryant, and FF DIN

Distributed in Canada by Raincoast Books
9050 Shaughnessy Street
Vancouver, British Columbia, V6P 6E5

10 9 8 7 6 5 4 3 2

Chronicle Books LLC
680 Second Street
San Francisco, California 94107

www.chroniclebooks.com

a l'Eva

Contents

Introduction

• • •

Paella is Spain's most famous and cherished dish. It's full of ritual and myth, tricks and techniques, and strict rules (Never stir the rice! Never cover while cooking!), yet open to interpretation and argument about what it can or can't include. Paella is often at the center of family gatherings and village or even city fests, especially in Valencia and Catalunya, along Spain's Mediterranean coast. There are other traditional ways of cooking rice in Spain, but paella is the most dramatic. You may prefer a moist rice dish of rabbit and quail in the *cazuela* (casserole) or a soupy rice cooked with lobster in a pot-bellied *caldero,* but nothing is as impressive as a large paella. Tip a thin, eighteen-inch-wide pan of rice the color of antique gold, studded with black mussels, toward a hungry table and there *will* be oohs and aahs. Among rice dishes, paella is king. It's spectacular, memorable, and delicious—devastatingly so when done well.

I vividly remember my first paella. A decade ago I followed a Catalan woman named Eva home to Barcelona from graduate school in London. A few days after arriving, I found myself sitting around the table at her parents' house for the weekly family paella. Her mother, Rosa, was born in Barcelona, though Rosa's parents both came from a tiny village in the Valencian countryside. Rosa's mother died when Rosa was very young, and Rosa spent part of her childhood among aunts (on both sides) in the village while her father worked in his small Barcelona grocery store. The aunts battled for the girl's attention—and comforted her—with their paellas. For more than forty years now, Rosa has been making near-weekly paellas for her family. There is an open invitation—just call by Friday evening so that

enough shellfish can be bought in the market Saturday morning. *Cuantos mas seremos, mas reiremos,* goes Spanish thinking. "The more we will be, the more we will laugh." And the more we will be, the bigger the paella!

On that memorable afternoon, Rosa carried her signature shellfish paella into the dining room, and when she tipped it toward us, I burst into applause, which drew more attention than the gorgeous, baroque rice. Plates were passed down and heaped with rice, jumbo shrimp and sweet prawns called *cigalas,* soft strips of cuttlefish, and tiny clams with grains of rice nestled inside. The thin layer of slightly caramelized rice known as *socarrat* was scraped from the pan and divided. It all tasted even more sublime than it looked. The nuttiness of the cuttlefish mingled with the *sofrito* (a slow-cooked aromatic tomato base), and the seafood was fragrant with sweet, smoky *pimentón* (paprika) and saffron. It was, quite simply, perfection. My affair with paella had begun. And so did my life in Spain: I stayed and married Eva not long afterward.

The Spanish word for rice, *arroz,* and the Catalan and Valencian *arròs* are derived from the Arabic *ar-ruzz.* The Arabs introduced rice into Spain in the eighth century, at the beginning of their long rule on the Iberian peninsula. They planted it around Valencia, including the marshy edges of the Albufera, the freshwater lake on the south side of the city, slightly inland from the sea (the name comes from the Arabic for "lake," *al-buhaira*). When Jaume I entered the city in 1238–halfway through the 700-year-long Christian *reconquista*

of the country–he found rice fields abutting the city. Cultivation has continued there, focused around the Albufera. Today the rice fields along the silted-up edges of the lake are cut with eel-rich canals and produce the finest and most sought-after Spanish rice.

Vast irrigated orchards and verdant produce gardens, the *huertas* that Valencia is famous for, begin at the edges of the rice fields and radiate across the region. It was here in these *huertas* that paella was born. Rice was a basic staple and field workers prepared it with their garden vegetables–such as fresh beans, tomatoes, and artichokes–and the snails they found among the rosemary and thyme that grew wild. On lucky days, they added a freshly killed rabbit or duck, and on special occasions, they slaughtered a chicken. The rice dish, cooked in a wide, shallow pan over the embers of olive- or orange-tree branches, was called *arroz a la valenciana.* At the end of the nineteenth century, it was finally named *paella valenciana,* after the distinctive pan the rice was cooked in and the place from where it came.

Variations came later, drawn from available ingredients. There may be only one Valencian Paella (page 42), but there are countless other paellas, from the classic *marisco* (shellfish, page 48) and *mixta* (mixed shellfish and poultry, page 56), to combinations such as rabbit and artichokes (page 58) and pork ribs and turnips (page 62). Paella adapts well to a variety of seasonal ingredients, from fresh game in autumn to asparagus in spring. You can be creative. Why not add squid, sardines, rosemary, or wild mushrooms?

But what makes a paella authentic? I have heard an extreme few claim that a paella wasn't a true paella unless it was made with lime-rich water from Valencia. Others say that anything other than *paella valenciana* is simply *un arroz en una paella* ("a rice in a paella pan"). The first claim is far too narrow, and the second is just playing with words. A paella is a paella as long as a handful of key requirements are met. First, highly absorbent short- or medium-grain rice is at the center of the dish. A paella is a rice dish first and foremost, and the purpose of each cooking step and every ingredient is to flavor it. Second, it includes olive oil, has a *sofrito* base, and is tinted yellow with saffron. Third, and most important, it is cooked in a wide, flat paella pan. Apart from giving the rice its name, the pan's shape allows the rice to be cooked in a thin layer. This puts as much rice as possible in contact with the bottom of the pan, where the flavors lie, and also allows the rice to cook evenly, with the quick evaporation needed to obtain the paella's dry texture and separate, firm grains.

The basic technique for preparing a paella is fairly straightforward, allowing, of course, for personal preferences. One standard method goes like this: The chicken, rabbit, game, poultry, and/or seafood are browned in olive oil. Then the vegetables–green bell peppers, red bell peppers, green beans, artichokes perhaps, tomatoes for certain–are added and slowly cooked down into a pulpy *sofrito*. Sweet *pimentón* is added and then the water. Saffron is sprinkled in, the liquid is brought to a boil, and when everyone is present, the rice is added.

The rice cooks, uncovered, for 10 minutes over high heat, then 8 more over lower heat until it is *al punto,* "at the point," with just a bite to it. After the paella is removed from the heat and covered, it rests for a few minutes before being served. Paella is an *arroz seco* (a "dry rice" dish), which means that the liquid must be completely absorbed at the precise moment that the rice is *al punto.* And here lies the challenge in a shifting equation of pan, heat source, and liquid.

Paellas can be extravagant or everyday simple. They may include the most expensive seafood or the cheapest sardines. In Spain, however, they are only eaten for lunch and never for dinner. And they are never prepared for one; two is the minimum. (Most restaurant menus explicitly state this.) Paellas are almost infinitely expandable (in 1992 the city of Valencia prepared a paella for 100,000 people) and they are perfect for gatherings of family or friends. In urban areas and for smaller families or groups, paella is usually made inside. For aficionados, though, it retains its rustic roots and is made and eaten outdoors.

The ideal and most time-honored method of preparing paella in the open air is over burning wood, with its sense of festivity. The outdoor paella in Spain remains largely the protected domain of men, who savor their moment of epicurean glory. Dishes of Marcona almonds and green olives are set out as groups hover about. They might be talking passionately of politics and *fútbol* (soccer), but all are keenly following the progress of the paella. Finally, when everyone is at last present (and never before), the rice is added. "*¡Veinte minutos!*" the shout goes out. Twenty minutes, and the rice will be ready.

Custom, harking back to the *huertas,* dictates that the paella be eaten directly from the pan. Everyone sits around the pan and works from his or her edge toward the center with a spoon. The pan is scraped clean, fruit is brought out, and then a light dessert. Strong coffee is prepared, and the afternoon slowly unfolds under the lengthening shade of a fig tree or the side of an old stone farmhouse among the wisps of lingering smoke and the smell of dry loam. Talk peters out and small groups break off to stroll quietly, or perhaps prepare another *cortado* (espresso with a dash of milk). Pass the day like this and you see how well the paella fits the Spanish character, and why it remains such a national favorite.

But paella is not the only traditional rice dish cooked in Spain. Rice is more commonly prepared in a *cazuela,* a thick, shallow casserole usually made of terra-cotta. *Cazuela* rice dishes and paellas have many similarities. The general approach to both is the same. The rice is the central ingredient, and everything else is added, including seasonal ingredients, to give the grains flavor. The rice is cooked for the same length of time and is always firm, never mushy.

But the *cazuela* mostly is what the paella is not. Cooking rice in a *cazuela* is essentially easier, without paella's strict rules (you can stir the rice) and the need for an abnormally wide heat source. A *cazuela* fits perfectly over a standard stove-top burner. Though

a *cazuela* rice dish is at the center of many family gatherings, it is more of an everyday, homey dish. The thickness of the *cazuela* offers even, consistent cooking, perfect for winter when it is nice to linger in the kitchen and let ingredients stew just a bit longer before adding the rice. *Cazuelas* are slower to heat than paella pans but also slower to cool, retaining their heat. That means the rice comes to the table hot—another benefit in winter. (Paella pans cool quickly when taken off the heat, and by the time the rice is rested and served, it is lukewarm.)

The finished texture of the rice is also different. Whereas paella rice is dry, *cazuela* rice tends to be moist, even soupy. More liquid is used, and since a *cazuela* pan has less surface area than a paella, less evaporates in the time it takes to cook the rice. *Cazuelas* have a flexibility that paellas don't have. If you want the rice more moist, just add in a bit more water or stock. It's as easy as that.

At the point that a finished rice dish is so moist that you need a spoon, it is considered a *caldoso.* The name derives from *caldo,* broth, and there should be at least a bit of that in each spoonful. That's a pretty broad definition, but everybody likes a different level of "soupy."

Some of my favorite rice dishes are soupy ones, such as Soupy Rice with Lobster (page 120), made with a dense fish stock and finished with a pounded paste of almonds, garlic, and sweet dried red peppers called *ñoras*; and Soupy Rice with Duck and Chanterelles (page 118). There are few greater pleasures than these on a cool weekend.

Although regular *cazuelas* work well for these soupier rices, the ideal cooking vessel is a tall-sided *cazuela,* similar to a Dutch oven, or better, a pot-bellied *caldero. Calderos* are high-sided pots that are slightly tapered at the mouth. Usually made of cast iron these days, rather than the traditional terra-cotta, they cook evenly and are perfect for long stewing.

Another very pleasurable rice dish to slow-cook on an autumn or winter Sunday when you have little desire to leave the house is *Arroz con leche* (page 130). Literally, "rice with milk," this creamy and slightly chewy rice pudding is fragrant with orange and lemon peels and cinnamon. It is one of Spain's best known and most loved desserts, its ultimate comfort food. The dish is also one of the few that preserve the ancient tradition of sweet rices. The thirteenth-century Hispano-Arabic *Anonymous Andalusian Cookbook* offered recipes for cooking rice with milk and honey or sugar and garnishing with almonds. Today, though, rice in Spain is almost exclusively a savory dish.

I have eaten plenty of paellas over the past ten years. We live within walking distance of my in-laws' flat and have been frequent guests for the weekend paella. I learned to eat and appreciate paella in that Barcelona flat and on the breezy terrace of their summer beach flat south of city, the yellow awning wound down against the sun. I have eaten it elsewhere, too, of course: in Barcelona and along the Catalan coast, but mostly when we are in Valencia. There we search it out in the many excellent rice restaurants and we enjoy it in the homes of my mother-in-law's competitive aunts. It is

a dish I never tire of eating. I never tire of its variations or even the repetition of my mother-in-law's shellfish paella, because that same dish is, in some way, always different—and always magical.

From the beginning of my life in Barcelona, my wife and I have made *cazuela* rices, and we have made these often. But the ritual of making a paella at home ourselves came later, once we had daughters of our own. Rosa eventually shared her method, and I gradually pieced together her recipe. One Christmas she drew my name to be my "secret Santa" and gave me my own paella pan. I love carrying out the paella from the kitchen myself, hearing the oohs and aahs (if I am lucky), then choosing who gets the choicest pieces (usually those who ooh and aah the loudest). Plates are passed down and dished up, and we dig in with great pleasure.

A NOTE ON LANGUAGE: *I have largely retained Spanish throughout for the sake of uniformity, except in a few instances where the Catalan word is relevant and/or of interest. It should be noted that the name for the Catalan language spoken in Valencia is Valencian.*

Basics

• • •

THE FOUR KEY ELEMENTS

ONE: THE PAN

The pan defines the rice. A paella is named for the pan in which it is cooked. A dish made of similar ingredients but cooked in a different pan is *un arroz* in Spanish, or *un arròs* in Catalan, and not a paella. The distinction is clear and unbending. Paellas are considered "dry" rice dishes; those cooked in *cazuelas* tend to be more moist, and those cooked in *calderos* are soupy.

La paella

The paella pan is wide and shallow and made of thin, conductive metal, with sloping sides and two handles. This shape facilitates a number of important things: The rice can be cooked in a thin layer (½ to ¾ inch thick), which allows for the even, simultaneous cooking of all the grains and for much of the rice to be in contact with the bottom of the pan, where the flavors from the *sofrito* lie. The shape of the pan also allows for maximum evaporation while the rice is cooking, which is crucial in getting the desired dry texture. The pan heats quickly and cools quickly. When it's removed from the heat, the rice in the bottom quits cooking almost immediately. Paellas do not have lids.

The word *paella* means "pan" in Catalan. The word derives from the Latin word *patella,* which means a plate or metal receptacle. The paella pan is often erroneously called a *paellera,* which has provoked heated debates. The Spanish rice authority Lourdes March, in the best-known Spanish book on rice, *El llibro de la paella y de los arroces,* is emphatic that the pan is called a *paella* and not a *paellera.* Period. Lorenzo Millo, the great Valencian food writer and author of a number of standard texts on Valencian cuisine, agrees. *Paellera* is the outdoor place where the paella is prepared over wood, as well as the woman who makes the paella (a man would be a *paellero*).

SIZES The amount of rice determines the size of the pan that is needed. The more rice the wider the pan, so that the rice layer remains thin. When everything is in the pan, the level of the liquid should ideally reach the pan's handles.

PAELLA PAN SIZES	
2 to 3 people	12" (30 cm) pan
2 to 4 people	14" (36 cm) pan
4 to 5 people	16" (40 cm) pan
4 to 6 people	18" (46 cm) pan
6 to 8 people	20" (50 cm) pan
10 people	22" (55 cm) pan
12 people	24" (60 cm) pan
15 people	26" (65 cm) pan

Most homes do not have pans to fit every numerical possibility or occasion, and so cooks adapt. "Where four can eat, so can five," is the philosophy of the Spanish table. The same with the paella pan. A 16-inch (40-centimeter) pan may be ideal for four to five, but it can be pressed into accommodating six. However, do not stretch pans more than a serving or two beyond the recommended number, or the whole purpose of using a paella pan is defeated. For a big group and a moderate-sized pan, another alternative is to reduce the amount of rice per person to ⅓ cup (instead of ½ cup) and serve hearty appetizers and a substantial salad.

THE CHOICE OF MATERIALS Paella pans are made to respond quickly to a change in heat. A paella is cooked over high heat for the first 10 minutes, then at a lower temperature for the next 8 minutes, and finally removed and rested before serving. As noted earlier, when the pan is taken off the heat, the rice on the bottom stops cooking almost immediately.

In Spain, most paella pans are made of polished carbon steel (*acero pulido*). The metal is thin and extremely heat-responsive. The pan gives a slightly sweet, metallic tang to the rice that for many is part of the paella's signature taste. The metal also reacts with certain vegetables, such as artichokes and eggplant, and gives them a darker (and some would argue unpleasant) tone.

Polished carbon steel pans are inexpensive but require the most care. Before you use one for the first time, you will need to season it: Simmer a mixture of equal parts water and vinegar in the pan for 5 to 10 minutes, and then wash it well with soap and water to remove the factory varnish. Next, boil a few handfuls of rice in plenty of fresh water for 5 to 10 minutes. Discard the rice, and wash the pan again. Once you have dried it, the pan is ready to use. It should always be dried immediately after washing. Before you store a carbon-steel pan, wipe it down with vegetable oil. Then, before using it again, simply sprinkle the oily pan with salt, gently warm, wipe clean, then wash with soap and water. Instead of oiling the pan for storage, it can also be dusted with flour, which will absorb some of the humidity and stop any oxidation in the pan, which will give the rice a rancid, rusty flavor.

More expensive, but much easier to care for, are pans made of stainless steel (*acero inoxidable,* often abbreviated as *inox*). These are also responsive to changes in heat on the stove top and work nicely. Because they are much easier to take care of and don't rust, they are especially good for those who make paella only occasionally.

A third option is a *paella esmaltada,* a steel pan coated with black-and-white speckled enamel. These are as easy to clean and care for as stainless steel but cost a fraction of the price, generally not much more than a polished carbon-steel pan.

Nonstick pans are to be avoided. They tend to be thicker, and thus slower and less responsive to heat changes. But the real reason to avoid them is you *want* the rice to stick, at least a bit, so that a slightly caramelized *socarrat* can form (see page 38).

There are two well-known stalls along the outside of Valencia's main Mercado Central (Central Market) that have been selling paella pans—and every possible burner, stand, tool, accessory, and complement for paella and rice making—for the better part of a century. Most of the paella pans they sell are either polished carbon or enameled steel. For cooking over wood, they both recommend only polished steel; for cooking on the stove top, they recommend enameled pans. In the end, though, the material of the pan matters less than the strength, size, and evenness of the heat source (see page 36 for a discussion on heat sources).

WHEN YOU DON'T HAVE A PAELLA PAN In a pinch, you can substitute one or two large skillets for a paella pan. Avoid cast iron or other heavy skillets that retain heat too long; stainless steel or aluminum are preferable. A 12-inch skillet will accommodate rice for two to three; two can handle enough rice for six. If you are using two skillets, cook the meats and the *sofrito* in a single pan. Then divide them between the skillets, add half the liquid to each, and carry on with the recipe.

La cazuela

The *cazuela* (*cassola* in Catalan) is a wide and shallow casserole without handles, though not as wide or shallow as a paella. *Cazuelas* are used for cooking almost everything in the Spanish kitchen. They distribute and retain heat well and are perfect for simmering and braising and producing moist, or even soupy, rice dishes on the stove top.

The size of the *cazuela* is less important than that of a paella pan. The ingredients should come at least one half to three fourths the way up the side, and even just below the lip is fine. The most common sizes are 12 inches (30 centimeters) for four people and 13 inches (32 centimeters) for six.

Cazuelas made of terra-cotta are by far the most common. These distinctive earthen red, kiln-fired casseroles are inexpensive and durable, and, if treated well, can last for years. Before using for the first time, soak the *cazuela* in water overnight (it should be completely submerged), and dry well. *Cazuelas* should be heated slowly, and are best used over low or medium heat. Do not place a hot *cazuela* on a marble countertop, or a cold *cazuela* (with, say, leftovers to be reheated) on a hot burner. These are surefire ways of cracking it.

Sturdier cast-aluminum and cast-iron *cazuelas* work equally well and are more practical. They have two loop handles on the sides for carrying the dish to the table, and there is no risk of cracking them. Le Creuset makes an enameled cast-iron shallow casserole called a "buffet casserole" that comes in various sizes. The Catalan company Castey makes shallow casseroles of thick cast aluminum triple coated with Teflon; they fall between terra-cotta and cast iron in weight, durability, and price. These are extremely popular locally and can be found in most good *ferreterías* (hardware stores) around Catalunya. Dutch ovens are also good substitutes for *cazuelas,* followed by large heavy skillets or saucepans. *Cazuelas* can also be found with tall sides, similar to a Dutch oven. These are perfect for soupier rices.

El caldero

The *caldero* (literally "caldron"; *calderó* in Catalan) is a heavy cast-iron or terra-cotta pot shaped like a stubby, slightly rounded lamp shade. These offer extremely uniform heat and are perfect for soups, stews, and soupy rices. They are most typical along the Murcian coast south of Valencia, where they were traditionally set directly on the fire. The tapered shape keeps the flames from leaping upward and licking the rice. The best known in Spain are Guisón (manufactured by the Valencian company Garcima, makers of the hugely popular La Ideal brand paella pans). They come in 2-liter, 5-liter, and 10-liter sizes, and are extremely heavy. With everything added, the ingredients should reach two thirds of the way up the side.

Dutch ovens, tall-sided *cazuelas,* and large heavy saucepans work well for soupier *caldoso* rice dishes.

TWO: THE RICE

Spanish rice dishes are first and foremost about rice. It is the protagonist. The rice needs to be able to absorb and conduct flavor; it is crucial to use either short- or medium-grain rice, preferably Spanish. Never use long-grain or parboiled rice, which do not absorb as much liquid as short- or medium-grain varieties.

The standard serving is ½ cup (100 grams) of uncooked rice per person. If the paella contains a lot of meats or seafood, or if it follows a number of appetizers, this amount can be reduced to ⅓ cup per person. The standard serving for soupy rices is ⅓ cup per person. The portions in this book are full portions, and the rice dishes are meant to be eaten as main dishes.

Spanish Varieties

Spanish short- and medium-grain rices are thick, pearled, and opaque. They absorb a lot of liquid while remaining firm. Short-grain rice, also known as round-grain, is shorter than one-fifth of an inch (5.2 millimeters) in length, and has a slight tail at one end. Medium-grain rice is between one-fifth and a quarter of an inch (5.2 to 6 millimeters). Both have a high degree of pearling. That's the concentration of starch in the middle of the grain that gives the rice its brilliant white color, allows for a lot of absorption, and lends a creaminess to the rice after cooking. The two sizes taste the same.

Short-grain Bomba is the most famous of the Spanish rice varieties. It is roughly three times more expensive in the supermarket than medium-grain varieties, and accounts

for nearly all of the exported Valencian rice. Bomba is less likely than a medium-grain rice to "open" and therefore lose its consistency or flavor when overcooked. For this reason, Bomba is usually recommended for novice paella makers.

Rice is grown in the Spanish regions of Valencia, Catalunya (namely the Ebro Delta on the border with Valencia), Murcia, Aragón, Navarra, Extremadura, and Andalucía (namely along the lower Guadalquivir River south of Sevilla). Three of the most important production areas have their own regulatory *denominacíon de origen* (often referred to by its abbreviation, D.O.), a registered designation of origin similar to the French wine *appellation d'origine contrôlée*. It controls the origin and varietal purity of the rice and monitors the production and harvesting. When buying, look for a D.O. label.

The most famous and sought-after D.O. rice is Arroz de Valencia. More than 90 percent of the D.O.'s area is around the Albufera Nature Park, just south of Valencia, where rice was initially introduced 1,200 years ago, mainly around the towns of Sueca, Sollana, Cullera, and Silla. Eight thousand farms working some 45,000 acres harvest roughly 20 percent of Spain's total rice production. There are just three varieties grown under the D.O. label, medium-grain Senia and Bahía, and, to a much lesser extent, short-grain Bomba. Brand names include La Fallera, La Campana, La Perdiz, Dasca, El Cazador, J. Montoro, Santo Tomas, Signo, and Ancora, though any with the D.O. certification is recommended.

The Arroz del Delta del Ebro D.O. is in the southern Catalan province of Tarragona. Jutting out like an arrow dozen of miles into the Mediterranean, the delta is the sprawling mouth of the Ebro River, the ancient Iberus River that gave the Iberian peninsula its name. Some sources date the earliest rice cultivation here by Benedictine monks to 1607 at Carrova, which acted as a base for spreading rice cultivation through the immediate area. The D.O. includes about 50,000 acres of canal-gridded land and draws in the municipalities of Amposta, San Jaume d'Enveja, San Carles de la Rápida, L'Aldea, Camarles, Deltebre, and L'Ampolla. Four varieties of medium-grain rice are cultivated, Bahía (foremost), Senia, Sequial, and Tebre.

Arroz de Calasparra is the third, and by far smallest, D.O., whose rice dates back to the fifteenth century. There are just under 3,000 acres available, but only 1,500 of them are planted each year. (The fields are alternated with cereals.) The D.O. land is a narrow strip along the Segura River and its main tributary, the Mundo River, in the provinces of Murcia and Albacete. Whereas the rice in Valencia and the Ebro Delta is grown at sea level in standing water, Calasparra rice is grown in valleys between 1,000 and 1,600 feet above sea level with cold, moving river water. These conditions form a harder grain, which needs a bit more water and time when cooking (see below). A medium-grain Balilla-Sollana cross and, to a lesser extent, the short-grain Bomba are grown here. Ninety-five percent of the D.O. rice produced in this zone is cultivated by the 160-member Cooperativa del Campo Virgen de la Esperanza, which sells both varieties of rice in distinctive white cloth bags with bold red lettering.

Non-Spanish Options

Other rices that work well in Spanish rice dishes include CalRiso, Calrose, California Blue Rose, Japanese short-grain rice, and superfine-grade Italian rices such as Carnaroli, Vialone Nano, and (especially for moist rices) Arborio.

Cooking Times

The rice must be combined with boiling liquid. There are two distinct schools of thought on how to do this: According to the first method, the cook adds the rice to liquid already boiling in the pan. Using the second approach, the cook adds the rice to the *sofrito*, lets it fry for a moment, and then adds boiling liquid to the pan, covering the rice. Those that favor the latter argue that rice allowed to fry briefly in the *sofrito* has more flavor. Too much frying, however, can form a sheen of oil around the grain and hinder its absorption of the liquid.

Regardless of which method you prefer, the texture of the grain is critical to the success of a rice dish. The rice should not be overcooked once it has been combined with the liquid. When rice is cooked too long, it opens, accordion-like, losing its firmness as well as its aroma.

Rice takes about 18 minutes to cook. It cooks for 10 minutes over high heat, and an additional 8 minutes over low heat, or until the liquid is absorbed and the rice has just a firm bite to it. The rice is removed from the heat, covered, and rested before serving. If you are cooking in a *cazuela*, the rice will continue to cook as long as it is in the pan, so serve it immediately and let it rest on plates instead.

For Bomba rice, increase the amount of liquid slightly and lengthen the cooking time by 1 minute. For rice from Calasparra, increase the liquid and the cooking time by 2 minutes. (For quantities, see the chart on page 25.)

THREE: THE BASES

Two keys to the tastiness of Spanish rice dishes are the *sofrito,* added at the beginning to give the dish structure and to flavor the liquid, and the *picada,* added at the end to give the food body and round out the flavors, particularly in *cazuela* and *caldero* rice dishes.

El sofrito

The foundation of nearly every rice dish is a *sofrito* (*sofregit* in Catalan), a slow, aromatic sauté of vegetables that includes one or more of the following: onions (though usually not in paellas), green or red peppers, garlic, and tomatoes. Other ingredients, including vegetables and cuttlefish or squid, can be incorporated into the mixture. The ingredients are added in a certain order and slowly cooked into a pasty, almost sweet base.

In drier rice dishes like paellas, onions aren't generally used in the *sofrito* because they can make the rice mushy, but in the more moist *cazuela* and *caldero* rice dishes, onions are almost always coupled with tomatoes. The onion usually leads off the *sofrito* and is cooked until soft and nearly translucent, about 5 to 10 minutes.

Green peppers, with their distinct and fragrant smell, are a typical addition. Spanish green peppers are long and thin with a tapered end. Green bell peppers are excellent substitutions. Red bell peppers are also used, adding color and sweetness to the rice. Finely chopped garlic can be added, too, usually with the tomatoes.

Tomatoes are often the main component of the *sofrito* and are always the last item added. They need to be fresh and ripe, fragrant and soft. They are peeled, seeded, and finely chopped before being added. Or you can grate them with a box grater, which is easier. Simply cut the tomato in half crosswise, and run a finger through the seed cavity, scraping most of the seeds out. Then, cupping the tomato in your hand, slowly grate. The skin will gradually peel back as the flesh is grated away, leaving only a flattened skin in your palm. (Discard the skin.) This technique doesn't waste precious pulp. In winter when good, flavorful fresh tomatoes are hard to find, canned whole tomatoes can be used. Strain them, reserving the liquid (to add later to the cooking *sofrito*), and finely chop.

The tomato is cooked over medium-low heat until its moisture has evaporated, its pulp has darkened, the taste has lost its acidity, and the texture is squishy. This will take about 10 to 15 minutes, though the time depends on the ripeness of the tomato.

A *sofrito* cannot be rushed. Times vary from pan to pan. Cooking the tomato down may take significantly less time in a paella pan, with its ampleness, than in a *cazuela.* Never leave a *sofrito* unattended; watch that it does not dry out and burn, which is more likely to happen in a paella pan. If it begins to dry out, add a few tablespoons of broth, water, or, if using canned tomatoes, the reserved tomato juice, as needed.

During cooking, while stirring, tap the onion and tomato with the flattened end of a wooden spoon to break them down into a creamy texture.

La picada

Whereas the *sofrito* leads, the *picada* finishes. Garlic, flat-leaf parsley, nuts, even the liver of a rabbit are pounded or ground into a fine, vaguely gritty paste and stirred into the rice toward the end of the cooking time. A *picada* draws the flavors together, gives them body and boldness, and changes the texture, and even the color, of the rice. *Picadas* are used more in *cazuela* and *caldoso* rice dishes than in paellas.

The *picada* (from the verb *picar,* "to chop") is traditionally pounded in a mortar. The pounding releases the flavors without destroying them, and allows complete control of the final texture of the *picada*. The classic Catalan mortar is yellow ceramic that comes with a hardwood pestle called *la ma,* "the hand." Alternatively, the *picada* can be ground in a food processor. Use quick on/off pulses, checking between each one, to achieve the desired texture.

That final texture should be very fine. In rice dishes the *picada* should be noticed only by its hint of flavors and not by pieces of garlic or nuts. A few tablespoons of water or stock added when pounding or grinding helps achieve that desirable smoothness.

One of the *picada*'s key ingredients is garlic, long a fundamental part of the Mediterranean diet. It can be added raw as long as enough cooking time remains to smooth out its bite and dominating taste. Or it can be sautéed in olive oil until pale gold in the opening step of preparing the rice. This flavors the oil as well as intensifying the garlic. But it is a process that needs to be watched closely; the point at which browning garlic turns bitter arrives quickly. (If this happens, discard the garlic, thoroughly clean the pan, and start again.)

Fresh flat-leaf parsley is another *picada* staple. Chop the parsley finely with a knife before pounding it in the mortar with the other *picada* ingredients.

Nuts, too, are typical. Almonds add an earthy flavor to the *picada,* and hazelnuts, even more so. A small handful is enough. Use toasted nuts with their skins slipped off.

For earthier tones, as in Hunter's Rice with Rabbit and Quail (page 108), sauté the liver of a rabbit and add it to the *picada*. The same can be done with the duck's liver in Soupy Rice with Duck and Chanterelles (page 118).

FOUR: THE LIQUID

Rice absorbs the liquid and acts as the final conductor of flavor. If the rice dish is made with only a few simple ingredients, a good, flavorful stock is crucial. In rices dishes where there is plenty of poultry, rabbit, pork ribs, game, or shellfish, as well as a good *sofrito,* water is enough to make a rich and flavorful liquid. But even rices with plenty of meats or seafood and a rich *sofrito* will be improved by a good stock. Simply said, the better the stock is, the better the rice will be, and time spent making one will be amply rewarded. The stock recipes that follow are without garlic or wine, and have only a small amount of salt.

In some recipes the raw materials themselves can be cooked to make a quick, simple stock. The neck and backbone of a disjointed chicken can be simmered in a pot with a few vegetables. The liquid from cooking clams can be used, too. In the pursuit of concentrated flavors, nothing is wasted; everything goes into the pot.

If you are using canned stock or broth, use only a low-sodium one. Instant bouillon cubes tend to be highly salty, and I don't recommend them.

The exact rice-to-liquid ratio varies, depending on the size of the pan, the heat source, and exactly how dry (or moist) you want the rice. A large paella pan with a thin layer of rice will evaporate more water than a *cazuela.* Similarly, a specially-made, wide paella gas-ring will evaporate more water in the time it takes to cook the rice than will a less potent stove-top burner. Take into consideration, too, evaporation during any prolonged stewing time before the rice is added.

APPROX. RICE/LIQUID PROPORTIONS

Dry paella rice   1 cup rice to 2 to 2½ cups liquid

Moist cazuela *rice*   1 cup rice to 3 cups liquid

Soupy caldoso *rice*   1 cup rice to 4 cups liquid

NOTE: *Increase the amount of water slightly for Bomba rice and rice from Calasparra*

Always keep a little bit of water or stock simmering on the stove to add to the rice in case all of the liquid has evaporated before the rice is *al punto.* For paellas, shake the liquid, tablespoon by tablespoon, over the parts where the rice looks less done (the grains will be whiter). *Cazuela* and *caldoso* rices are more flexible than paellas, and liquid can be added with ease to reach the desired moistness.

Fish Stock

MAKES 8 CUPS | Each 1 pound of fish heads and bones, plus some vegetables, makes 4 cups of rich, tasty stock. Avoid vigorously boiling the fish; the goal is to simply extract the essence and aromas of the sea.

1 tablespoon extra-virgin olive oil
1 medium onion, roughly chopped
1 carrot, cut into 10 or so pieces
2 pounds heads and bones of monkfish or another white fish
1 celery rib, cut into thirds
10 sprigs fresh flat-leaf parsley
12 peppercorns
½ teaspoon salt
9 cups water

In a stockpot, Dutch oven, or another large heavy pot, heat the oil over medium heat. Cook the onion and carrot until they begin to brown and release their juices, about 5 minutes. Add the fish heads and bones, celery, parsley, peppercorns, salt, and water. Bring almost to a boil, then reduce the heat and simmer, partly covered, for 30 minutes.

Strain and reserve the stock, discarding the solids.

To store the stock, let cool, then cover and refrigerate for up to 2 days or freeze for up to 3 months.

Chicken Stock

MAKES 8 CUPS | Use a cleaver to chop up the chicken. For a stock that is lower in fat, let cool, refrigerate until well chilled, and scrape off the accumulated layer of fat from the surface.

1 tablespoon extra-virgin olive oil

2 pounds chicken thighs or legs, roughly chopped

1 medium onion, roughly chopped

1 carrot, cut into 10 or so pieces

½ medium turnip (about 3 ounces), halved

1 celery rib, cut into thirds

10 sprigs fresh flat-leaf parsley

1 bay leaf (optional)

12 peppercorns

½ teaspoon salt

8½ cups water

In a stockpot, Dutch oven, or another large heavy pot, heat the oil over medium heat. Cook the chicken, onion, and carrot until they begin to brown, about 5 minutes. Reduce the heat to low and cook for another 5 minutes, until the carrot and onion release their juices. Add the turnip, celery, parsley, bay leaf, peppercorns, salt, and water. Bring to a boil, then reduce the heat and simmer, covered, for 45 minutes.

Strain and reserve the stock, discarding the solids.

To store the stock, let cool, then cover and refrigerate for up to 4 days or freeze for up to 3 months.

Vegetable Stock

MAKES 8 CUPS | This is a good stock to have on hand if there are vegetarians in your family.

1 tablespoon extra-virgin olive oil
1 medium onion, roughly chopped
1 large leek (white and green parts), roughly chopped
2 carrots, cut into 10 or so pieces
1 medium turnip, quartered
1 celery rib, cut into thirds
1 medium potato, peeled and quartered
10 sprigs fresh flat-leaf parsley
12 peppercorns
½ teaspoon salt
8½ cups water

In a stockpot, Dutch oven, or another large heavy pot, heat the oil over medium heat. Cook the onion, leek, and carrots until they begin to brown and release their juices, about 5 minutes. Add the turnip, celery, potato, parsley, peppercorns, salt, and water. Bring to a boil, and then reduce the heat and simmer, covered, for 1 hour.

Strain and reserve the stock, discarding the solids.

To store the stock, let cool, then cover and refrigerate for up to 4 days or freeze for up to 3 months.

OTHER KEY INGREDIENTS

OLIVE OIL

Use extra-virgin olive oil, which handles the heat well during the cooking process and is easier to digest. A mild one is best. A thin film of oil that covers the bottom of the pan is sufficient. Too much oil can coat the rice grains and impede their ability to absorb the liquid, which will mean less flavorful rice.

SALT

Salt opens up flavors—don't be afraid of it. Begin with two healthy pinches when adding the tomatoes to the *sofrito*. Taste just before adding the rice, and adjust the seasoning as needed. Beyond this, the amount of salt is not specified in these recipes. There are too many variables, including personal preference, whether a stock is used (and how salty it is), and the type of salt you are adding. Sea salt and kosher salt are both recommended.

SAFFRON

Saffron is a defining element of paella. It brings its characteristic warm and fresh aroma, and, significantly, tints the rice a delicate golden color. It is the world's most expensive spice. Cultivation is a delicate process, collecting is difficult, and it takes some 70,000 flowers to yield a pound of saffron. Introduced into Spain around A.D. 900 by Arab traders, it was cultivated in Spain by A.D. 960. (The Spanish word for saffron, *azafrán,* comes from the Arabic *za'faran.*) Saffron is largely grown in the central La Mancha region, whose extreme conditions—hot summers, cold winters—are ideal for giving strength to the color and pungency to the aroma. La Mancha is a registered *denominación de origen*; look for the "D.O. Azafrán de la Mancha" label. Buy only threads and not powder, which may have been adulterated.

To draw out saffron's full culinary potential, the threads need to be slightly toasted and crumbled before they are added to a rice dish. Toast the threads in a small dry skillet over low heat for a few minutes until they turn a shade darker. Remove them immediately, and then either crumble them in a small piece of paper or pound them in a mortar. If using a mortar, be sure to swirl a bit of water around inside after pounding to get every last bit of saffron dust.

Most restaurants, and many home cooks, use a powdered *colorante* (usually a mix of cornstarch, salt, and yellow dye) to give their paella the dish's characteristic golden color. Though eschewed by purists, *colorante* does not carry a heavy stigma in Spain and its use is not generally looked down upon around most tables. *Colorante* gives the rice an artificially bright yellow tone. Do not try to make a paella yellower by simply adding more saffron. Too much saffron can give the rice a bitter, almost medicinal flavor. Two pinches of good-quality threads—20 to 30 total—is enough for a paella for 6.

PIMENTÓN

There are three kinds of Spanish *pimentón* (paprika): *dulce* (sweet), *agridulce* (bittersweet

or semisweet), and *picante* (hot). Paella requires the sweet variety, which is the most typical *pimentón* in Spain. It's silky, fine, and blood-red with a deep, smoky flavor. *Pimentón* is delicate and burns quickly in the pan, becoming bitter. I like to add it at the end of the *sofrito,* stirring it in for a few seconds to let the flavors meld before quickly adding the liquid to the pan.

Peppers were perhaps first grown in Spain at the Monastery of Guadalupe near La Vera, Extremadura, in the southwest, sometime after Columbus himself presented samples there in 1493. They became popular and spread through Spain and then Europe, notably to Hungary.

La Vera remains the heart of the Spanish *pimentón* industry. The peppers are dried and then slowly smoked over oak logs in carefully controlled, low-slung smokehouses; then they are slowly milled. Production in La Vera is regulated by a D.O. Murcia also produces excellent *pimentón.*

SNAILS

Snails were probably first cultivated in Spain by the Romans. They are essential ingredients to a number of paellas, including the original *Paella valenciana* (page 42).

When using snails in rice dishes, smaller is better. The most popular variety, the vineyard snail (*Helix pomatia*), which is the typical French escargot and is called *de les vinyes* or *vinyal* in Valencia and Catalunya, is simply too large for the paella pan. The common snail (*Helix aspersa*), known as *petit-gris* in France, and *bover* or *moro* in Valencia and Catalunya, is smaller and preferable. Even smaller and tastier are ones called *vaquetes* in Valencia. But the best (though hard to find outside of Valencia) are even smaller white snails with distinctive chocolate-brown whirls called *chonetes* (*Eobania vermiculata,* chocolate-band snails).

Snails can be bought precooked and preserved in brine at certain specialty shops, such as the Spanish Table (see Sources, page 134). These are perfectly acceptable, though live snails are preferable. Most live snails bought in Spanish or U.S. markets are ready to use immediately, and don't need to be fed herbs and bran and then purged of their impurities as they once did.

Before preserved, precooked snails are added to the rice, they should be rinsed, boiled for 3 to 4 minutes in plenty of water, and then rinsed again. Live snails need to be cooked slowly with herbs and vegetables over low heat for an hour, drained, and then rinsed (see Note, page 45). The snails are then added into the *sofrito* to allow them time to absorb the flavors and lend their own to the rice.

MUSHROOMS

Mushrooms are abundant and appreciated in many parts of Spain, including Catalunya and Valencia, where they are routinely collected in the wild. The majority of mushrooms, though, are bought in the market. Some of these are wild, but most have been cultivated. In such meccas as Petràs Fruits del Bosc in Barcelona's La Boqueria market, the selection is extensive and changes throughout the seasons.

The list of Spanish favorites that are available in U.S. markets include cèpes, morels, chanterelles, trumpets of death, and white button mushrooms. Other excellent choices include oyster mushrooms, portobellos, and shiitakes. For these recipes, buy whatever is freshest and looks the best in the market.

How and even whether to clean mushrooms always causes debate. Llorenç Petràs, the owner and namesake of the famed La Boqueria stall, recommends simply brushing or wiping off mushrooms found in the forest and washing those bought in the market. To wash, drop them into a sink full of cold water, swish them around (the grit will sink), change the water, and repeat the process a couple of times. Don't let mushrooms soak in water or wash them too long before using.

The mushrooms are cooked first in a separate pan and then added to the rice just before it is done. One technique I learned from Petràs is cooking the mushrooms over moderately low heat so that moisture is expelled but isn't immediately evaporated. The liquid is later added to the rice. The cooking time varies, depending on the type of mushroom, but as a general rule cook them slowly for around 5 minutes until the liquid has been expelled, then drain it off and reserve. Increase the heat and quickly sauté the mushrooms for 2 minutes to give the edges a brown tint and sweeter flavor.

RABBIT

The mild, flavorful white meat of rabbit is a traditional and delicious ingredient commonly found in paellas. Young rabbits, weighing 2 to 2½ pounds, are preferable. Buy the rabbit whole and reserve the liver to use in the *picada*. Use a cleaver or large, sharp knife to cut the rabbit into pieces. Carefully pick out any bone shards from the meat before adding it to the pan.

SHRIMP AND PRAWNS

Shrimp classified as "jumbo" (11 to 15 per pound) and "colossal" (10 or fewer per pound) are often called prawns in the United States, but prawns are a different species. The most common prawns cooked in Spanish rice dishes are Dublin Bay prawns, which are called *cigalas* in Spanish and *escamarlans* in Catalan. They are also known as Norway lobsters and by their plural Italian name, *scampi*. Resembling miniature lobsters, they are 4 to 8 inches long, orange colored, and have oversized elongated pincers. The shells are tough and the meat is sweet. If you cannot find prawns, use colossal shrimp. Buy whole raw shrimp or prawns with their heads and shells still on.

CUTTLEFISH AND SQUID

The sweet, nutty flavor of these chewy cephalopods is crucial to numerous rice dishes. Either can be used, as the flavor and texture are similar.

Generally speaking, a cuttlefish—*sepia* in Spanish, *sípia* or *sèpia* in Catalan—resembles a large squid. It is meatier, slightly more tender, and a bit more flavorful than squid, and is ideal

for cutting into thin strips. It is sold fresh and also frozen as cuttlefish steaks. Squid—*calamar* in Spanish and Catalan—is equally excellent. Use the tentacles as well as the body tube, which can be cut into strips or rings.

When buying fresh squid or cuttlefish, look for whole ones with their heads intact. They need to have a clear, fresh, sea-briny smell. When cleaning, reserve the ink sacs to use in *Arròs negre amb allioli* (Black Rice with Allioli, page 78). To clean, pull out the head

and entrails. Carefully remove the ink sac(s) found beneath the tentacles, and reserve. Trim off the tentacles and reserve, discarding the rest. Remove the hard, clear quill from inside the tube and any innards that remain.

Packets of squid ink can be bought at select stores, including Italian and Asian markets.

TECHNIQUES FOR EXCELLENT PAELLAS

PAELLA'S FOUR GOLDEN RULES

1. Do not wash the rice first.
2. Do not add the rice until everyone is present. (People will wait for rice, but rice will wait for no one.)
3. Do not stir the rice.
4. Do not cover while cooking the rice.

HEAT SOURCES: STOVES, GRILLS, BURNERS, AND WOOD

A wide paella pan needs a wide, powerful, and uniformly distributed source of heat that can accommodate the pan and cook the rice evenly. A good heat source, or an understanding of how to manipulate what you have, is key to a successful paella.

For many, the most common place to cook a paella is on a kitchen stove top. But the standard burner is tiny compared to a large paella pan. The pan, then, needs to be steadily rotated over one, two, or even, for a very large pan, three burners to assure even cooking. If straddling more than one burner, it is easier to sauté the meats or seafood and cook the *sofrito* over a single burner in the center of the pan. Then set it astride two or three burners when the liquid is added. The cooking time may be slightly longer. Keep a small amount of water or broth simmering on the stove to add as needed.

A preferable, and relatively inexpensive, option for gas stoves is an extension that fits into the burner. These offer wide bands of uniform heat and come in various sizes. They are difficult to find in the United States, but make a perfect item to buy if visiting Spain (see Sources, page 135).

Another option is to cook the paella outside on a charcoal or gas grill. With this method I find it easier to sauté the meats and seafood and prepare the *sofrito* in a skillet on the stove top inside, and then transfer them to the paella pan on the grill outside. Add the liquid, bring it to a boil, add the rice, and carry on with the recipe.

Perhaps the best way to cook a large paella outdoors is using a freestanding butane or propane burner mounted on a sturdy set of legs. These emit a good, strong flame. Sizes vary and can accommodate very large pans.

Cooking a paella over a wood fire is the most romantic and also the most traditional option. It accommodates a large paella pan, and the smoke seasons the rice slightly with its sweet aroma. In Valencia, the branches of orange or olive trees are the preferred fuel. Short-legged wood fire stands that straddle the burning logs or embers are inexpensive and come in a variety of sizes. The trick is ensuring even cooking for the entire pan.

FINISHING THE PAELLA IN THE OVEN

Some cooks like to finish the paella in the oven, arguing that it produces a drier dish. Others argue this is a restaurant-style shortcut that is against the rustic spirit of the dish. (The rebuttal to this is, simply, If it makes a better

paella, so what?) Such a technique works only, of course, if the paella pan is smaller than the width of the oven. With its handles, an 18-inch pan is almost 23 inches wide.

To finish a paella in the oven, preheat the oven to 400°F. Cook the paella over high heat on the stove top for 10 minutes, then slide it into the hot oven for the final 10 minutes or so, until the liquid is absorbed and the rice is just about done. Some cover the pan with foil when placing it in the oven, especially if the rice is a bit dry. Once the pan is removed from the oven, cover it with paper towels and let the paella rest as usual before serving.

SOCARRAT

Socarrat is the slightly caramelized crust that forms on the bottom of the pan. It is not burnt! This somewhat chewy rice is prized, and scraping it from the pan is a noisy joy—a moment when a boxwood spoon is appreciated. *Socarrat* forms in a well-cooked paella. Some try to form it by increasing the heat to high for the final 2 minutes or so, but there is a risk of burning the rice, and it should be watched very carefully if attempted.

AL PUNTO

Al punto ("at the point") is when rice reaches that important moment of doneness and the pan needs to be removed immediately from the heat. The rice has just a bite to it, and the hard bright white nucleus has nearly disappeared. A grain broken in half will show a single tiny dot of white. It will finish cooking during the resting period.

RESTING THE PAELLA BEFORE SERVING

When the rice is *al punto* the paella is removed from the heat, covered, and rested for 5 minutes before serving. This lets the rice finish cooking, especially the grains on the top, and the flavors round out. The starches firm up and will hold their shape when served. Paper towels are the easiest way to cover the paella, though a clean kitchen towel works, and even sheets of newspaper will work. Rest the paella in a warm place; it should be neither hot nor cold.

SERVING

The serving sizes in this book are full servings. A paella is intended to be the main dish. Serve it with a simple green salad, garnished with olives, crescents of sliced onions, and fresh tomatoes, and dressed with extra-virgin olive oil, a couple of dashes of vinegar, perhaps, and a pinch of salt.

As I have noted earlier, a paella is traditionally set in the middle of the diners and everyone eats directly from the pan. You start at your own edge and work toward the middle, using a spoon made from boxwood. A number of rice restaurants in Valencia will set the paella in the middle of the table and, if asked, provide wooden spoons. At home forget the wooden spoon if you want (nearly everyone nowadays does), but try eating the paella out of the pan with a regular spoon. This is done not just to follow tradition, but because it is a nice way to eat paella and people enjoy doing it.

If you are serving on plates, do not dish out the paella in the kitchen. Bring the whole pan to the table, tip it toward your family and friends (to oohs and aahs), then have the plates passed down to you. The paella maestro, *el paellero* or *la paellera,* decides who gets the choicest pieces—the meatiest pieces of monkfish, the largest shrimp, the front legs of the rabbit. It is a not-so-subtle way of showing who is in favor (and who is not). After you have made a great paella, no one will begrudge you this small privilege of power.

PREPARING AHEAD

Paellas and other rice dishes can be made ahead successfully to the point just before the rice is added. The meats and seafood can be fried, the *sofrito* prepared, and even the liquid added, *but don't add the rice!* If it is a few hours before or even the day before you want to serve, let the mixture cool, then cover and refrigerate it. If it's only a matter of hours, add the liquid, turn off the heat, and cover with aluminum foil to avoid evaporation. When you're ready to finish cooking, simply remove the foil, bring the liquid to a boil, add the rice, and carry on as usual.

INCREASING AND DECREASING QUANTITIES

Paellas are very flexible and easy to scale up or down. There are only two points to remember: the rice-to-liquid ratio always remains constant, while the size of the pan changes.

Quien arroz come, buenos carrillos pone.

"Whoever eats rice gets nice cheeks."

Paellas

Paella valenciana
The Original Valencian Paella

SERVES 6 | *Paella valenciana* does not have a precise recipe—it was born in the fields and not in a chef's restaurant kitchen—but there is an accepted ingredients list. This recipe is adapted from the official one used in Sueca's nearly fifty-year-old annual paella competition, held in the Albufera village of Sueca each year, and approved by town government as well as the Club of Head Chefs of the Community of Valencia. The only additions here are some herbs to make the snails tastier.

Paella valenciana famously uses different types of fresh beans, namely *garrofó* (lima beans), *tavella* (a type of long white bean), and *ferraúra* (a local green bean). Fresh lima beans are shucked from the pod, but the white beans and green beans are not; their pods are cut into short sections. Lima beans can be hard to find fresh, and canned or frozen are acceptable. Dried lima beans need to be soaked and boiled before adding to the paella. Fresh white beans can also be difficult to find (look in Italian and French markets); again, dried ones need to be soaked and boiled before adding. You can also do what Spanish cooks do: use the fresh beans that look best in the market.

1 pound chicken thighs or legs, cut into 8 to 10 pieces

½ rabbit (about 1 pound), cut into 6 to 8 pieces

Salt

6 tablespoons extra-virgin olive oil

½ pound shucked fresh lima beans

¼ pound fresh small white beans in their pods, ends trimmed, and cut into 2-inch-long sections

½ pound green beans, ends trimmed, and cut in half

2 garlic cloves, finely chopped

2 ripe medium tomatoes, peeled, seeded, and finely chopped or coarsely grated (see page 23)

36 live or preserved snails, cooked (see Note, page 45), or 1 sprig fresh rosemary

1 teaspoon sweet *pimentón*

8 cups water

2 pinches saffron threads (about 20 total), lightly toasted and ground (see page 30)

3 cups short- or medium-grain rice

continued →

Paella valenciana

Season the chicken and rabbit generously with salt. In a 16- to 18-inch paella pan, heat the oil over medium heat. Add the chicken and rabbit and cook, stirring frequently, until browned, about 5 minutes. Add all the beans and cook until they begin to soften, about 5 minutes. Reduce the heat to medium-low, add the garlic, tomatoes, and 2 pinches of salt and cook, stirring from time to time, until the tomato has darkened to a deeper shade of red, 10 to 15 minutes. Stir in the snails (if using), sprinkle in the *pimentón,* and add the water. Bring to a simmer, and continue simmering for 10 minutes, or until the meat and beans are tender.

Add the saffron and (if you are not using snails) the rosemary. Taste for salt and adjust the seasoning as needed. Increase the heat to high and bring to a boil. Sprinkle in the rice. With a wooden spoon, probe the pan to make sure the rice is evenly distributed. Do not stir again. Cook, uncovered, for 10 minutes over high heat, then reduce it to low and cook for an additional 8 minutes, or until the liquid is absorbed and the rice is *al punto,* with just a bite to it.

Remove the paella from the heat, cover with paper towels, and let rest for 5 minutes before serving.

NOTE: *If using live snails, clean the shells well and put in a medium saucepan. Add 1 quartered tomato, 1 quartered onion, 1 teaspoon sweet or bittersweet* pimentón, *1 sprig fresh rosemary, and 1 small handful fresh mint. Cover with abundant cold water and slowly bring to a boil. Reduce the heat to low and simmer for 1 hour. Drain the snails, rinse, and set aside.*

If using preserved snails, rinse, put in a medium saucepan, cover with abundant water, and boil for 3 to 4 minutes. Drain, rinse, and set aside.

Paella a la marinera
Fishermen's Paella

SERVES 6 | This paella celebrates the flavors of Spain's coasts, mixing both shellfish and fish. Monkfish, with its sublime flavor and firm flesh, is ideal, though any other firm-fleshed white fish will work well. Use what looks best and freshest at the market.

8⅓ cups water

½ pound small clams, purged of sand (see Note)

Salt

½ pound mussels, scrubbed and debearded

1 pound monkfish steaks, or 10 ounces grouper fillets, or another firm-
  fleshed white fish steak or fillet, deboned and broken into pieces

Freshly ground pepper

6 tablespoons extra-virgin olive oil

Flour for dredging

1 green bell pepper, cored, seeded, and cut into 1-inch-square pieces

1 pound cuttlefish or squid, cleaned and cut into 2-by-½-inch pieces (see
  page 35)

18 large raw head-on shrimp with shells

1 garlic clove, finely chopped

4 ripe medium tomatoes, peeled, seeded, and finely chopped or coarsely
  grated (see page 23)

½ teaspoon sweet *pimentón*

2 pinches saffron threads (about 20 total), lightly toasted and ground
  (see page 30)

3 cups short- or medium-grain rice

In a medium saucepan, bring 5 cups of the water to a boil and add the clams and a pinch of salt. Reduce the heat and simmer, partly covered, for 30 minutes. Remove from the heat and set aside, covered, leaving the clams in the water. (Discard any that do not open.)

Meanwhile, put the mussels in a small sauté pan, add ⅓ cup of the water, and bring to a boil. Reduce the heat and simmer, uncovered, until all of the mussels have opened, 3 to 5 minutes. Remove from the heat and set aside, covered. Do not drain. (Discard any that do not open.)

Season the fish generously with salt and pepper. In a 16- to 18-inch paella pan, heat the oil over medium heat. When the oil begins to shimmer, dredge the fish, piece by piece, in flour and then cook in batches, turning just once, until golden on the outside and just cooked through in the middle. Transfer to a platter.

Remove any solids left in the oil with a skimmer or slotted spoon and then prepare the *sofrito* in the same pan. Add the bell pepper, and cook, over medium heat, stirring frequently, until it begins to brown and become fragrant, about 3 minutes. Add the cuttlefish and cook until its moisture has been expelled, about another 5 minutes, stirring constantly and scraping anything that sticks to the pan. Add the shrimp and cook until pink, about 2 minutes on each side. Lower the heat to medium-low, add the garlic, tomatoes, and 2 pinches of salt, and cook, stirring from time to time, until the tomato has darkened to a deeper shade of red and the *sofrito* is pasty, 10 to 15 minutes.

Meanwhile, strain the broth from the clams and reserve it. Discard one shell (the empty one) from each clam, and set aside the rest.

When the *sofrito* is ready, sprinkle in the *pimentón* and saffron, letting the flavors meld for a few seconds while stirring constantly. Add 4 cups of the reserved clam broth plus the remaining 3 cups of water, increase the heat to high, and bring to a boil. Taste for salt and adjust the seasoning as needed. Sprinkle in the rice. With a wooden spoon, probe the pan to make sure the rice is evenly distributed. Do not stir again. Lay the pieces of fish on top and then the shrimp. Cook, uncovered, for 10 minutes over high heat. Reduce the heat to low and cook for an additional 8 minutes, or until the liquid is absorbed and the rice is *al punto,* with just a bite to it.

Remove the paella from the heat, cover with paper towels, and let rest for 5 minutes before serving.

NOTE: *To purge clams of sand, soak in cool water with 2 pinches of salt for at least 30 minutes.*

Paella de marisco de Rosa

Rosa's Shellfish Paella

SERVES 6 | My mother-in-law Rosa's signature paella offers a beautiful bounty of flavors from the sea. For decades she has been making it with the same care and attention to details, never rushing it and only using the finest and freshest ingredients. When I think of a paella, this is what I imagine. It remains, for me, simply the best.

7⅓ cups water

½ pound small clams, purged of sand (see Note, page 47)

Salt

½ pound mussels, scrubbed and debearded

6 tablespoons extra-virgin olive oil

1 green bell pepper, cored, seeded, and cut into 1-inch-square pieces

1 pound cuttlefish or squid, cut into 2-by-½-inch pieces (see page 35)

12 to 18 large raw head-on shrimp with shells

6 raw head-on prawns (see page 34) or colossal shrimp with shells

4 ripe medium tomatoes, peeled, seeded, and finely chopped or coarsely grated (see page 23)

½ teaspoon sweet *pimentón*

2 pinches saffron threads (about 20 total), lightly toasted and ground (see page 30)

¼ cup fresh or thawed frozen peas

2½ cups short- or medium-grain rice

In a medium saucepan, bring 5 cups of the water to a boil and add the clams and a pinch of salt. Reduce the heat and simmer, partly covered, for 30 minutes. Remove from the heat and set aside, covered, leaving the clams in the water. (Discard any that do not open.)

Meanwhile, put the mussels in a small sauté pan, add ⅓ cup of the water, and bring to a boil. Reduce the heat and simmer, uncovered, until all of the mussels have opened, 3 to 5 minutes. Remove from the heat, and set aside, covered. Do not drain. (Discard any that do not open.)

Prepare the *sofrito*. In a 16- to 18-inch paella pan, heat the oil over medium heat. Add the bell pepper and cook, stirring frequently, until it begins to brown and become fragrant, about 3 minutes. Add the cuttlefish and cook until browned and its moisture has been

continued →

expelled, about another 5 minutes, stirring constantly and scraping anything that sticks to the pan. Add the shrimp and cook until pink, about 2 minutes on each side. Lower the heat to medium-low and add the prawns, tomatoes, and 2 pinches of salt and cook, stirring from time to time, until the tomato has darkened to a deeper shade of red and the *sofrito* is pasty, 10 to 15 minutes.

Meanwhile, strain the broth from the clams, and reserve it. Discard one shell (the empty one) from each clam and set aside the rest.

When the *sofrito* is ready, sprinkle in the *pimentón* and saffron, letting the flavors meld for a few seconds while stirring constantly. Stir 4 cups of the reserved clam broth plus the remaining 2 cups of water into the paella, and add the clams and peas. Simmer for 10 minutes. Taste for salt and adjust the seasoning

as needed. Remove the prawns and transfer to a platter. Increase the heat, return the mixture to a boil, and sprinkle in the rice. With a wooden spoon, probe the pan to make sure the rice is evenly distributed. Do not stir again. Cook, uncovered, for 10 minutes over high heat. Reduce the heat to low and cook for an additional 8 minutes, or until the liquid is absorbed and the rice is *al punto,* with just a bite to it. Remove from the heat, cover with paper towels, and let rest for 5 minutes.

Return the prawns to the paella, laying them on the rice. Drain the mussels and discard one shell (the empty one) from each mussel. Arrange the mussels in their remaining shells decoratively around the pan so they are pointing downward. Serve.

50

Paella de pescado

Fish Paella

SERVES 6 | This fish paella can be made using one type of fish or several. You can also use a combination of steaks and fillets. If you can find a medium-sized whole monkfish, buy it. Use the head for the stock and the rest for the rice.

1½ to 2 pounds mixed steaks or fillets of monkfish, sea bream, grouper,
    scorpion fish, redfish, sea bass, or another firm-fleshed white fish
Salt and freshly ground pepper
6 tablespoons extra-virgin olive oil
Flour for dredging
1 green bell pepper, cored, seeded, and cut into 1-inch-square pieces
1 pound cuttlefish or squid, cleaned and cut into 2-by-1-inch pieces
    (see page 35)
2 garlic cloves, finely chopped
4 ripe medium tomatoes, peeled, seeded, and finely chopped or coarsely
    grated (see page 23)
1 teaspoon sweet *pimentón*
2 pinches saffron threads (about 20 total), lightly toasted and ground
    (see page 30)
7 cups Fish Stock (page 26)
3 cups short- or medium-grain rice
¼ cup fresh or thawed frozen peas (optional)

Season the fish generously with salt and pepper. In a 16- to 18-inch paella pan, heat the oil over medium heat. When the oil begins to shimmer, dredge the fish, piece by piece, in flour and then cook in batches, turning just once, until golden on the outside and just cooked through in the middle. Transfer to a platter.

Remove any solids left in the oil with a skimmer or slotted spoon and then prepare the *sofrito* in the same pan. Add the bell pepper and cook over medium heat, stirring frequently, until it begins to brown and become fragrant, about 3 minutes. Add the cuttlefish and cook until browned and its moisture has been expelled, about another 5 minutes, stirring constantly and scraping anything that sticks to the pan. Add the garlic, tomatoes, and 2 pinches of salt and cook, stirring from time to time, over medium-low heat until the tomato

continued →

has darkened to a deeper shade of red and the *sofrito* is pasty, 10 to 15 minutes.

Meanwhile, debone the steaks if desired, break the fillets into pieces, and discard all bones and skin.

When the *sofrito* is ready, sprinkle in the *pimentón* and saffron, letting the flavors meld for a few seconds while stirring constantly. Add the stock, increase the heat, and bring to a boil. Taste for salt and adjust the seasoning as needed. Sprinkle in the rice and peas, if using. With a wooden spoon, probe the pan to make sure the rice is evenly distributed. Do not stir again. Cook, uncovered, for 5 minutes over high heat. Distribute the cooked pieces of fish evenly around the pan. Continue to cook over high heat for another 5 minutes, then reduce the heat to low and cook for an additional 8 minutes, or until the liquid is absorbed and the rice is *al punto,* with just a bite to it.

Remove the paella from the heat, cover with paper towels, and let rest for 5 minutes before serving.

Paella de pescado azul

Bluefish Paella

SERVES 6 | In Spain, anchovies, sardines, mackerel, herring, and small tuna are loosely referred to as *pescado azul,* literally, "blue fish." This is an informal rather than scientific grouping. The fish are linked by their dark meat, silver backs, and high amount of healthy omega-3 fatty acids.

1 pound fresh sardines, herring, mackerel, tuna, smelt, or a mixture of
 several

Salt and freshly ground pepper

6 tablespoons extra-virgin olive oil

Flour for dredging

1 green bell pepper, cored, seeded, and cut into 1-inch-square pieces

3 medium artichokes, trimmed, tough parts of leaves removed, cut into
 eighths, and choke scraped out

2 garlic cloves, finely chopped

4 ripe medium tomatoes, peeled, seeded, and finely chopped or
 coarsely grated (see page 23)

1 teaspoon sweet *pimentón*

2 pinches saffron threads (about 20 total), lightly toasted and ground
 (see page 30)

7 cups Fish Stock (page 26)

3 cups short- or medium-grain rice

¼ cup fresh or thawed frozen peas

Remove the heads, tails, and entrails of the fish. Leave the fish that are no bigger than small sardines whole, and cut the larger ones into 1- to 2-inch pieces. Rinse with fresh water and pat dry with a paper towel. Season generously with salt and pepper. In a 16- to 18-inch paella pan heat the oil over medium heat. When the oil begins to shimmer, dredge the fish, piece by piece, in flour and cook in batches until golden on the outside and just about cooked through in the middle, turning carefully to avoid breaking the skin. Transfer to a platter.

Remove any solids left in the oil with a skimmer or slotted spoon and then prepare the *sofrito* in the same pan. Add the bell pepper and artichokes, reduce the heat to low, and cook until they begin to brown, about 5 minutes.

continued →

Add the garlic, tomatoes, and 2 pinches of salt, raise the heat to medium-low and cook, stirring from time to time, until the tomato has darkened to a deeper shade of red and the *sofrito* is pasty, 10 to 15 minutes.

When the *sofrito* is ready, sprinkle in the *pimentón* and saffron, letting the flavors meld for a few seconds while stirring continually. Add the fish stock, increase the heat, and bring to a boil. Taste for salt and adjust the seasoning as needed. Sprinkle in the rice and peas. With a wooden spoon, probe the pan to make sure the rice is evenly distributed. Do not stir again. Cook, uncovered, for 10 minutes over high heat. Reduce the heat to low, lay the fish atop the rice, and cook for an additional 8 minutes, or until the liquid is absorbed and the rice is *al punto,* with just a bite to it.

Remove the paella from the heat, cover with paper towels, and let rest for 5 minutes before serving.

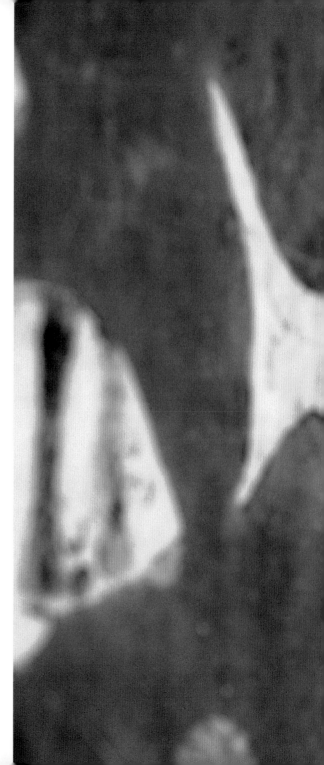

Paella mixta

Mixed Poultry and Seafood Paella

SERVES 6 | Mixing meats and seafood is common in parts of Spain. This paella draws on the disparate sea and land flavors of clams, mussels, shrimp, pork, and chicken, and brings them together in a full-flavored melange. It is, understandably, one of the most popular paellas.

9⅓ cups water

½ pound small clams, purged of sand (see Note, page 47)

Salt

½ pound mussels, scrubbed and debearded

1 pound pork spareribs, ribs cut apart and chopped into ¾-inch pieces

1 pound chicken thighs or legs, cut into 8 to 10 pieces

Freshly ground pepper

6 tablespoons extra-virgin olive oil

12 large raw head-on shrimp with shells

1 pound cuttlefish or squid, cleaned and cut into 2-by-½-inch pieces
    (see page 35)

2 garlic cloves, finely chopped

4 ripe medium tomatoes, peeled, seeded, and finely chopped or coarsely
    grated (see page 23)

1 teaspoon sweet *pimentón*

2 pinches saffron threads (about 20 total), lightly toasted and ground
    (see page 30)

3 cups short- or medium-grain rice

In a medium saucepan, bring 5 cups of the water to a boil and add the clams and a pinch of salt. Reduce the heat and simmer, partly covered, for 30 minutes. Remove from the heat and set aside, covered, leaving the clams in the water. (Discard any that do not open.)

Meanwhile, put the mussels in a small sauté pan, add ⅓ cup of the water, and bring to a boil. Reduce the heat and simmer, uncovered, until all of the mussels have opened, 3 to 5 minutes. Remove from the heat, and set aside, covered. Do not drain. (Discard any that do not open.)

Season the pork ribs and chicken generously with salt and pepper. In a 16- to 18-inch paella pan, heat the oil over medium heat.

Add the pork and chicken and cook, stirring frequently, until browned, about 5 minutes. Transfer to a large platter. Add the shrimp to the pan and cook until pink, about 2 minutes on each side. Transfer to the platter.

Remove any solids left in the oil with a skimmer or slotted spoon and then prepare the *sofrito* in the same pan. Add the cuttlefish and cook over medium heat, stirring and scraping anything that sticks to the pan, for 2 minutes. Add the garlic, tomatoes, and 2 pinches of salt and cook over medium-low heat, stirring from time to time, until the tomato begins to darken, about 5 minutes. Return the pork and chicken to the paella pan along with any juices from the platter, and cook, stirring from time to time, until the *sofrito* is pasty, about 5 minutes.

Meanwhile, strain the broth from the clams and reserve it. Discard one shell (the empty one) from each clam, and set aside the rest.

When the *sofrito* is ready, sprinkle in the *pimentón*, letting the flavors meld for a few seconds while stirring constantly. Add 4 cups of the reserved clam broth plus the remaining 4 cups of water, bring to a simmer, and simmer for 10 minutes.

Add the clams and the saffron. Taste for salt and adjust the seasoning as needed. Increase the heat to high and bring the liquid to a boil. Sprinkle in the rice. With a wooden spoon, probe the pan to make sure the rice is evenly distributed. Do not stir again. Lay the shrimp on top. Cook, uncovered, for 10 minutes over high heat. Reduce the heat to low and cook for an additional 8 minutes, or until the liquid is absorbed and the rice is *al punto*, with just a bite to it.

Remove the paella from the heat, cover with paper towels, and let rest for 5 minutes.

Discard one shell (the empty one) from each mussel, and arrange the mussels in their remaining shells decoratively around the pan, pointing downward. Serve.

Paella de conejo y alcachofas

Paella with Rabbit and Artichokes

SERVES 6 | Rabbit, with its delicious and tender meat, is commonly found in paellas. The artichokes and red peppers help weave an earthiness into the dish. To heighten that note, sauté the rabbit's liver with the meat and then pound it in a mortar with some almonds, and stir it into the paella when adding the rice.

> 1 whole rabbit (about 2 pounds), cut into about 12 pieces
>
> Salt and freshly ground pepper
>
> 6 tablespoons extra-virgin olive oil
>
> 6 medium artichokes (about 2 pounds), trimmed, tough parts of leaves removed, cut into eighths, and choke scraped out
>
> 1 red bell pepper, cored, seeded, and cut into 1-inch-square pieces
>
> 2 garlic cloves, finely chopped
>
> 4 ripe medium tomatoes, peeled, seeded, and finely chopped or coarsely grated (see page 23)
>
> 1 teaspoon sweet *pimentón*
>
> 8 cups Chicken Stock (page 28)
>
> 2 pinches saffron threads (about 20 total), lightly toasted and ground (see page 30)
>
> 3 cups short- or medium-grain rice

Season the rabbit generously with salt and pepper. In a 16- to 18-inch paella pan, heat the oil over medium heat. Add the rabbit and cook until browned, about 5 minutes. Transfer to a large platter.

Prepare the *sofrito* in the same pan. Add the artichokes and bell pepper and cook over medium heat for 5 minutes. Add the garlic, tomatoes, and 2 pinches of salt and cook, stirring from time to time, over medium-low heat until the tomato begins to darken, about 5 min-

utes. Return the rabbit to the paella pan along with any juices from the platter, and cook, stirring from time to time, until the *sofrito* is pasty, about 5 minutes.

When the *sofrito* is ready, sprinkle in the *pimentón*, letting the flavors meld for a few seconds while stirring constantly. Add the chicken stock, bring to a simmer, and simmer for 10 minutes.

Sprinkle in the saffron. Taste for salt and adjust the seasoning as needed. Increase

continued →

the heat to high and bring the liquid to a boil. Sprinkle in the rice. With a wooden spoon probe the pan to make sure the rice is evenly distributed. Do not stir again. Cook, uncovered, for 10 minutes over high heat. Reduce the heat to low and cook for an additional 8 minutes, or until the liquid is absorbed and the rice is *al punto,* with just a bite to it.

Remove the paella from the heat, cover with paper towels, and let rest for 5 minutes before serving.

61

Paella de costillas de cerdo y nabos

Paella with Pork Ribs and Turnips

SERVES 6 | This is an adaptation of the classic paella in Valencia called *fesols i naps,* "white beans and turnips." The original dish is flavored with the jowl, feet, ears, and fat of a pig, which I have replaced here with spareribs. In Spain, this dish is best in winter, when turnips are at their peak. The unpeeled garlic adds a robustness to the rice as well as a decorative touch, sitting in the middle of the paella like a flower. Rub off the papery outer skin of the garlic before adding it to the pan, but leave the head intact.

6 tablespoons extra-virgin olive oil

1 head unpeeled garlic, plus 1 peeled clove, finely chopped

½ green bell pepper, cored, seeded, and cut into 1-inch-square pieces

2 pounds pork spareribs, ribs cut apart and chopped into ¾-inch pieces

Salt and freshly ground pepper

4 ripe medium tomatoes, peeled, seeded, and finely chopped or coarsely grated (see page 23)

¾ pound turnips, peeled and cut into bite-size pieces

8½ cups water or Vegetable Stock (page 29)

1 teaspoon sweet *pimentón*

2 pinches saffron threads (about 20 total), lightly toasted and ground (see page 30)

3 cups short- or medium-grain rice

In a 16- to 18-inch paella pan, heat the oil over medium heat. Add the head of unpeeled garlic and cook for 2 minutes. Add the bell pepper and cook until brown and fragrant, about 4 minutes.

Season the ribs generously with salt and pepper, add to the pan, and cook until browned, about 5 minutes. Add the chopped garlic, tomatoes, and 2 pinches of salt, and cook, stirring from time to time, over medium-low heat until the tomato has darkened to a deeper shade of red and the *sofrito* is pasty, about 15 minutes.

Add the turnips and 1½ cups of the water and simmer until the liquid has evaporated and the ribs and turnips are tender, about 15 minutes.

continued →

Sprinkle in the *pimentón* and saffron, letting the flavors meld for a few seconds while stirring constantly. Add the remaining 7 cups of water, increase the heat to high, and bring to a boil. Check for salt, adjusting the seasoning as needed. Sprinkle in the rice. With a wooden spoon, probe the pan to make sure the rice is evenly distributed. Do not stir again. Cook, uncovered, for 10 minutes over high heat, then reduce the heat to low and cook for an additional 8 minutes, or until the liquid is absorbed and the rice is *al punto,* with just a bite to it.

Remove the paella from the heat, cover with paper towels, and let rest for 5 minutes before serving.

Paella de masia

Farmhouse Paella with Rabbit, Chicken, and Pork Ribs

SERVES 6 | A *masia* is a Catalan farmhouse, and this dish incorporates three classic Catalan farm flavors: rabbit, chicken, and pork. Add the rabbit's liver—cooked with the meat and pounded in the mortar—for deeper, fuller-bodied tones. It's a meaty, filling paella, so there is slightly less rice per person.

½ rabbit (about 1 pound), cut into 6 to 8 pieces

½ chicken (about 1½ pounds), cut into small pieces

½ pound pork spareribs, ribs cut apart and chopped into ¾-inch pieces

Salt and freshly ground pepper

6 tablespoons extra-virgin olive oil

1 red bell pepper, cored, seeded, and cut into 1-inch-square pieces

4 ripe medium tomatoes, peeled, seeded, and finely chopped or coarsely grated (see page 23)

2 garlic cloves, peeled

8 whole almonds, toasted (see Note, page 66)

1 teaspoon chopped fresh flat-leaf parsley

1 teaspoon sweet *pimentón*

7 cups water or Chicken Stock (page 28)

2 pinches saffron threads (about 20 total), lightly toasted and ground (see page 30)

2½ cups short- or medium-grain rice

Season the rabbit, chicken, and spareribs generously with salt and pepper. In a 16- to 18-inch paella pan, heat the oil over medium heat. Add the rabbit and chicken and cook until golden, about 5 minutes. Add the ribs and continue to cook until the meat is browned, about 4 minutes. Transfer to a platter.

In the same pan, prepare the *sofrito*. Add the bell pepper and cook over medium heat until brown and fragrant, about 5 minutes.

Add the tomatoes and 2 pinches of salt and cook, stirring from time to time, over medium-low heat until the tomato has darkened, about 5 minutes. Return the rabbit, chicken, and ribs to the pan along with any juices from the platter, and cook, stirring from time to time, until the *sofrito* is pasty, about 5 more minutes.

Meanwhile, prepare the *picada* by pounding in a mortar the garlic, almonds, and parsley with 2 tablespoons of water until you have a

continued →

fine paste. Or whir them in a food processor or blender (see page 24).

When the *sofrito* is ready, sprinkle in the *pimentón,* letting the flavors meld for a few seconds while stirring constantly. Add the water, bring to a simmer, and simmer for 10 minutes.

Sprinkle in the saffron. Taste for salt and adjust the seasoning as needed. Increase the heat and bring to a boil. Sprinkle in the rice and spoon in the *picada.* With a wooden spoon, probe the pan to make sure the rice is evenly distributed. Do not stir again. Cook, uncovered, for 10 minutes over high heat. Reduce the heat to low and cook for an additional 8 minutes, or until the liquid is absorbed and the rice is *al punto,* with just a bite to it.

Remove the paella from the heat, cover with paper towels, and let rest for 5 minutes before serving.

NOTE: *To toast whole raw almonds, preheat the oven to 400°F. If the almonds have skins, blanch in boiling water for 4 minutes, drain, and plunge into cold water. Drain, pile them on a paper towel, and rub until their skins slip off. Place the almonds on an ungreased baking sheet and bake, shaking the pan occasionally, until golden, crunchy, and fragrant, 10 to 12 minutes. Remove from oven and let cool.*

Paella de verduras

Garden Vegetable Paella

SERVES 4 | Vegetable paella is one of the classic paellas. Use whatever vegetables are in season—asparagus in spring, mushrooms in autumn, turnips in winter—and look freshest in the market. Vegetable paellas are just as adaptable to seasons, tastes, and whims as those with meat and seafood.

6 tablespoons extra-virgin olive oil

1 red bell pepper, cored, seeded, and cut into 1-inch-square pieces

1 medium eggplant, peeled and cut into ½-inch-dice

¼ pound green beans, ends trimmed and cut into 1-inch pieces

3 medium artichokes, trimmed, tough parts of leaves removed, cut into eighths, and choke scraped out

½ pound cauliflower, broken into bite-size pieces

9 tender garlic shoots, root ends trimmed, outer layers peeled away, and only the last inch used

2 garlic cloves, finely chopped

4 ripe medium tomatoes, peeled, seeded, and finely chopped or coarsely grated (see page 23)

Salt

6 cups Vegetable Stock (page 29) or water

½ teaspoon sweet *pimentón*

2 pinches saffron threads (about 20 total), lightly toasted and ground (see page 30)

⅓ cup fresh or thawed frozen peas

2 cups short- or medium-grain rice

In a 14- to 16-inch paella pan, heat 4 tablespoons of the oil over medium heat. Add the bell pepper and eggplant and cook until they begin to brown, about 5 minutes. Transfer to a plate. Add the remaining 2 tablespoons of oil to the pan, and then add the green beans, artichokes, and cauliflower and cook for 5 minutes. Lower the heat to medium-low, add both types of garlic, the tomatoes, and 2 pinches of salt, and cook, stirring from time to time, until the tomato has darkened to a deeper shade of red and the *sofrito* is pasty, 10 to 15 minutes. Add

1 cup of the stock and simmer until the liquid has evaporated and the vegetables are tender, about 10 minutes.

Return the bell pepper and eggplant to the pan. Sprinkle in the *pimentón* and saffron, letting the flavors meld for a few seconds while stirring constantly. Add the remaining 5 cups of stock and the peas, increase the heat, and bring to a boil. Taste for salt and adjust the seasoning as needed. Sprinkle in the rice. With a wooden spoon, probe the pan to make sure the rice is evenly distributed. Do not stir again. Cook, uncovered, for 10 minutes over high heat, then reduce the heat to low and cook for an additional 8 minutes, or until the liquid is absorbed and the rice is *al punto,* with just a bite to it.

Remove the paella from the heat, cover with paper towels, and let rest for 5 minutes before serving.

Paella de setas

Paella with Wild Mushrooms

SERVES 6 | This paella changes each time it's made, depending on what kinds of mushrooms can be found either in the woods or in the market. Autumn offers the largest selection, but spring has its gems (morels!). Choose the freshest mushrooms you can find, preferably a selection of three or four different types.

The liquid that the mushrooms expel during cooking is used to help flavor the rice. Be sure to cook them over medium-low heat so that the precious juice isn't evaporated.

6 tablespoons extra-virgin olive oil

4 ripe medium tomatoes, peeled, seeded, and finely chopped or coarsely
   grated (see page 23)

Salt

1 pound assorted wild mushrooms, cleaned (see page 34) and cut into
   pieces if caps are larger than 2 inches

2 garlic cloves, finely chopped

1 teaspoon sweet *pimentón*

2 pinches saffron threads (about 20 total), lightly toasted and ground
   (see page 30)

7 cups Vegetable Stock (page 29) or Chicken Stock (page 28)

3 cups short- or medium-grain rice

Prepare the *sofrito*. In a 16- to 18-inch paella pan, heat 4 tablespoons of the oil over medium-low heat. Add the tomatoes and 2 pinches of salt, and cook, stirring from time to time, until the tomato has darkened to a deeper shade of red and the *sofrito* is pasty, 10 to 15 minutes.

Meanwhile, heat the remaining 2 tablespoons of oil in a large sauté pan over medium-low heat and cook the mushrooms, garlic, and 2 more pinches of salt until the mushrooms have expelled their liquid, about 5 minutes. Drain and reserve the liquid. Increase the heat to high, and cook mushrooms and garlic for another 2 minutes. Transfer to a platter.

When the *sofrito* is ready, sprinkle in the *pimentón* and saffron, letting the flavors meld for a few seconds while stirring constantly. Add the vegetable stock plus the reserved broth from the mushrooms, increase the heat to high, and bring to a boil. Check for salt, adjusting the seasoning as needed. Sprinkle in the rice.

continued →

With a wooden spoon, probe the pan to make
sure the rice is evenly distributed. Do not
stir again. Distribute the mushrooms evenly
around the pan. Cook, uncovered, for 10 minutes over high heat, then reduce the heat to low
and cook for an additional 8 minutes, or until
the liquid is absorbed and the rice is *al punto*,
with just a bite to it.

Remove the paella from the heat, cover
with paper towels, and let rest for 5 minutes
before serving.

Paella de primavera

Spring Paella

SERVES 6 | This paella is a sibling of the *Paella valenciana* (page 42) from the *huertas*, the irrigated orchards and fields around Valencia. In spring they are bursting with fresh vegetables as well as snails. (See page 33 for more on snails.) If snails aren't in season a sprig of rosemary can be substituted.

¼ cup extra-virgin olive oil

½ green bell pepper, cored, seeded, and cut into 1-inch-square pieces

6 ounces green beans, ends trimmed and cut into 1-inch-long pieces

6 medium artichokes, trimmed, tough parts of leaves removed, cut into eighths, and choke scraped out

4 tender garlic shoots, root ends trimmed, outer layers peeled away, and only the last inch used

2 scallions (white and green parts), ends trimmed and roughly chopped

2 garlic cloves, finely chopped

4 ripe medium tomatoes peeled, seeded, and finely chopped or coarsely grated (see page 23)

Salt

8 cups Vegetable Stock (page 29) or Chicken Stock (page 28)

1 teaspoon sweet *pimentón*

2 pinches saffron threads (about 20 total), lightly toasted and ground (see page 30)

3 cups short- or medium-grain rice

½ pound live or preserved snails, cooked (See Note, page 45)

1 pound asparagus, bottoms trimmed

½ cup shelled fresh peas

Prepare the *sofrito*. In a 16- to 18-inch paella pan, heat the oil over medium heat. Add the bell pepper, green beans, artichokes, tender garlic, and scallions and cook, stirring frequently, until they begin to brown and soften, 5 to 10 minutes. Add the garlic cloves, tomatoes, and 2 pinches of salt and cook, stirring from time to time, over medium-low heat until the tomato has darkened to a deeper shade of red and the *sofrito* is pasty, 10 to 15 minutes.

continued →

Add 1 cup of the stock, bring to a simmer, and continue simmering until the liquid has evaporated, about 10 minutes.

When the liquid has evaporated in the *sofrito,* sprinkle in the *pimentón* and saffron, letting the flavors meld for a few seconds while stirring constantly. Add the remaining 7 cups of stock, increase the heat, and bring to a boil. Check for salt and adjust the seasoning as needed. Sprinkle in the rice. With a wooden spoon, probe the pan to make sure the rice is evenly distributed. Do not stir again. Cook, uncovered, for 5 minutes over high heat. Distribute the snails, asparagus, and peas evenly around the pan. Cook for another 5 minutes over high heat, then reduce the heat to low and cook for an additional 8 minutes, or until the liquid is absorbed and the rice is *al punto,* with just a bite to it.

Remove the paella from the heat, cover with paper towels, and let rest for 5 minutes before serving.

Arròs negre amb allioli

Black Rice with Allioli

SERVES 6 | This classic Catalan coastal rice dish is not only colored by the black cuttle-fish or squid ink, but also flavored by its tight, briny essence. The ink sac, of course, comes inside the squid, so when cleaning be sure to reserve it, or ask your fishmonger to do so. Ink can also be purchased in some specialty shops; 2 teaspoons is plenty. The flavor of the rice is mellow, almost sweet, and is perfect served with creamy garlic *Allioli*.

5 tablespoons extra-virgin olive oil

1 medium onion, finely chopped

1 red bell pepper, cored, seeded, and cut into 1-inch-square pieces

2 pounds cuttlefish or squid, cleaned and cut into bite-size pieces (see page 35), ink sac(s) reserved; or 1 pound cut-up cuttlefish or squid steaks and 2 teaspoons ink

4 ripe medium tomatoes, peeled, seeded, and chopped or coarsely grated (see page 23)

Salt

2 garlic cloves, peeled

7 cups Fish Stock (page 26)

1 teaspoon sweet *pimentón*

2 pinches saffron threads (about 20 total), lightly toasted and ground (see page 30)

3 cups short- or medium-grain rice

Allioli (page 81)

In a 16- to 18-inch paella pan, heat the oil over medium-low heat. Add the onion and bell pepper and cook until the onion is soft and translucent, 5 to 10 minutes. Add the cuttlefish and cook for 5 minutes, stirring and scraping anything that sticks to the pan. Add the tomatoes and 2 pinches of salt and cook, stirring from time to time, until the tomato has dark-ened to a deeper shade of red and the *sofrito* is pasty, 10 to 15 minutes.

Meanwhile, pound the garlic in a mortar. Add the ink sac(s) and a dash of fish stock and carefully mash with the garlic into a runny paste.

When the *sofrito* is ready, sprinkle in the *pimentón* and saffron, letting the flavors meld for a few seconds while stirring constantly.

continued →

Add the stock, increase the heat, and bring to a boil. Add the rice and spoon in the garlic-ink paste. Check for salt, adjusting the seasoning as needed. With a wooden spoon, probe the pan to make sure the rice is evenly distributed. Do not stir again. Cook, uncovered, for 10 minutes over high heat, then reduce the heat to low and cook for an additional 8 minutes, or until the liquid is absorbed and the rice is *al punto*, with just a bite to it.

Remove the paella from the heat, cover with paper towels, and let rest for 5 minutes before serving. Serve with *allioli* on the side in a bowl, encouraging people to dollop the sauce liberally on the rice.

Allioli

MAKES ¾ CUP, ENOUGH FOR 6 PEOPLE | *Allioli* is a compound of the Catalan words *all* ("garlic"), *i* ("and"), and *oli* ("oil"). Traditionally, it is only those ingredients. They are slowly pounded in a mortar into a thick emulsion. It's slow and laborious, and though some still make it that way, most add an egg and use a hand blender. These *minipimers* are the workhorse of the Spanish kitchen, performing innumerable tasks—including making *allioli*. (Braun, KitchenAid, Bamix, and Cuisinart are some of the brands that sell models in the United States.) The ideal container in which to prepare *allioli* is in the tall, cylindrical one slightly larger than the blender shaft. (It generally comes with the blender.) A food processor works, too; use quick on/off pulses to reach the desired texture.

This is my sister-in-law Rosa Maria's version. Whenever she comes for lunch, I ask her to make it. She prefers to use sunflower oil as it makes a lighter *allioli* than olive oil does. The two oils can be mixed, too, using half of each.

1 large garlic clove or 2 small ones, peeled

1 large egg at room temperature

¾ cup sunflower oil

⅛ teaspoon salt

In a tall, narrow, cylindrical container add, in this order, the garlic, egg, oil, and salt. Place the hand blender in the container so that the shaft touches the bottom, and begin to purée at about three-quarters of full speed. Keep the blender shaft in the bottom of the container until the ingredients start to thicken, then move it very slowly all the way up, and then down to the bottom and back up again.

The total blending time is about 45 seconds. The final consistency should be like thick mayonnaise.

Cover and refrigerate until ready to serve. It will keep for up to 2 days in the refrigerator.

Arroz a banda

Rice with the Fish Served Separately

SERVES 6 | This is one of the grandest *arrossos* in Catalunya, where it is called *arròs a banda*. The name literally means "rice apart." First the fish is cooked in the broth, and then the cooking liquid is used to also cook the rice. The two are then eaten separately. The potatoes and onions are served with the fish and therefore need to be cut into large pieces, so they don't disintegrate while cooking in the stock. The fish and potatoes are eaten liberally slathered in *allioli*.

6 tablespoons extra-virgin olive oil

2 medium onions, peeled and cut lengthwise into fourths

1 leek (white and green parts), cut into ½-inch pieces

3 small white potatoes, peeled and cut into ½-inch-thick rounds

1 pound heads and bones of monkfish or another white fish

Salt

8 cups water

1 garlic clove, peeled

16 whole almonds (about ½ ounce), toasted (see Note, page 66)

1 tablespoon chopped fresh flat-leaf parsley

1 pound mixed steaks or fillets of monkfish, sea bream, grouper, scorpion fish, redfish, sea bass, or other firm-fleshed white fish

Freshly ground pepper

4 ripe medium tomatoes, peeled, seeded, and finely chopped or coarsely grated (see page 23)

1 teaspoon sweet *pimentón*

2 pinches saffron threads (about 20 total), lightly toasted and ground (see page 30)

3 cups short- or medium-grain rice

Allioli (page 81)

Prepare the stock. In a stockpot, Dutch oven, or another large heavy pot, heat 2 tablespoons of the oil over medium heat. Add the onions, leek, and potatoes, and cook, stirring frequently, until they begin to brown and release their juices, about 5 minutes. Add the fish heads and bones and 2 pinches of salt, cover with the water, and bring to a boil. Reduce the heat to medium-low, and cook, partly covered, for 20 minutes.

While the stock simmers, prepare the *picada* by pounding the garlic, almonds, and parsley with 2 tablespoons of water in a mortar until you have a fine paste. Or whir them in a food processor or blender (see page 24).

Once the stock has simmered for 20 minutes, generously season the fish fillets with salt and pepper, and gently add them to the stock, and cook for another 10 minutes. Transfer the fillets and potatoes to a platter, and cover to keep warm. Strain the stock and set aside, discarding the solids.

While the fish is cooking, prepare the *sofrito*. In a 16- to 18-inch paella pan, heat the remaining 4 tablespoons of oil over medium-low heat. Add the tomatoes and 2 pinches of salt, and cook, stirring from time to time, until the tomato has darkened to a deeper shade of red and the *sofrito* is pasty, 10 to 15 minutes.

When the *sofrito* is ready, sprinkle in the *pimentón* and saffron, letting the flavors meld for a few seconds while stirring constantly. Add 7 cups of the fish stock, increase the heat, and bring to a boil. Check for salt, adjusting the seasoning as needed. Add the rice and stir in the *picada*. With a wooden spoon, probe the pan to make sure the rice is evenly distributed. Do not stir again. Cook, uncovered, for 10 minutes over high heat. Reduce the heat to low, and cook for an additional 8 minutes, or until the liquid is absorbed and the rice is *al punto*, with just a bite to it.

Remove the paella from the heat, cover with paper towels, and let rest for 5 minutes.

Moisten and warm the fish by spooning over it a bit of the remaining stock. Serve the rice and fish separately, but at the same time. Serve with *allioli* on the side.

Arroz a banda con gambas y ajo

Rice with the Shrimp and Garlic Served Separately

SERVES 6 | This is another rice dish with the two components served apart, this time shrimp and garlic. Watch very carefully that the garlic doesn't burn, or it will taint the entire dish. Use large whole shrimp with their heads on. To eat them, first pinch off each head, and gently squeeze it between your thumb and forefinger while sucking out the juice. The head is where the most concentrated flavors lie. Then you can peel the body and enjoy its sweet meat.

6 tablespoons extra-virgin olive oil

1 medium onion, roughly chopped

1 carrot, cut crosswise into 10 or so pieces

2 pounds heads and bones of monkfish or another white fish

1 celery rib, cut into thirds

10 sprigs fresh flat-leaf parsley

12 peppercorns

Salt

8 cups water

18 to 24 large raw head-on shrimp with shells

8 garlic cloves, thinly sliced

3 ripe medium tomatoes, peeled, seeded, and finely chopped or coarsely
   grated (see page 23)

½ teaspoon sweet *pimentón*

2 pinches saffron threads (about 20 total), lightly toasted and ground
   (see page 30)

3 cups short- or medium-grain rice

Prepare the stock. In a stockpot, Dutch oven, or another large heavy pot, heat 2 tablespoons of the oil over medium heat. Add the onion and carrot and cook until they begin to brown and release their juices, about 5 minutes. Add the fish heads and bones, celery, parsley, peppercorns, 2 pinches of salt, and the water.

Bring almost to a boil, then reduce the heat and simmer, partly covered, for 30 minutes. Strain the liquid and set aside, discarding the solids.

When the stock has simmered for almost 10 minutes, begin preparing the rice. In a 16- to 18-inch paella pan, heat the remaining

continued →

4 tablespoons of oil over medium heat. Add the shrimp and garlic and cook until the shrimp are done and the garlic is pale gold, about 4 minutes. Transfer both to a platter and cover to keep warm.

Remove any solids left in the oil with a skimmer or slotted spoon. Add the tomatoes and 2 pinches of salt and cook, stirring from time to time, over medium-low heat until the tomato has darkened to a deeper shade of red and the *sofrito* is pasty, 10 to 15 minutes.

When the *sofrito* is ready, sprinkle in the *pimentón* and saffron, letting the flavors meld for a few seconds while stirring constantly. Add the fish stock, increase the heat, and bring to a boil. Check for salt, adjusting the seasoning as needed. Sprinkle in the rice. With a wooden spoon, probe the pan to make sure the rice is evenly distributed. Do not stir again. Cook, uncovered, for 10 minutes over high heat. Reduce the heat to low and cook for an additional 8 minutes, or until the liquid is absorbed and the rice is *al punto,* with just a bite to it.

Remove the paella from the heat, cover with paper towels, and let rest for 5 minutes before serving.

Serve the rice and the platter of shrimp and garlic separately, but at the same time.

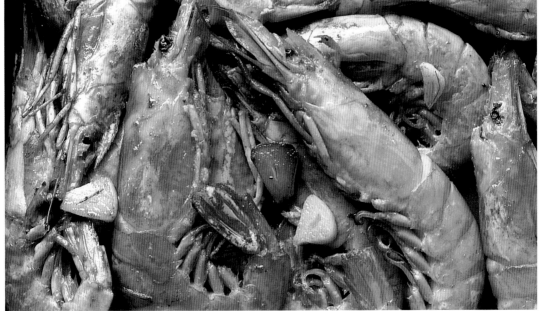

Arrossejat d'escamarlans

Catalan Toasted Rice with Prawns

SERVES 4 | Here the rice is browned first by toasting it in the paella pan before the fish stock is added. It's a simple dish, subtle and delicious. The heads of the prawns can be removed after frying and added to the stock. This takes away the joy of pinching them off and sucking them later, but it does give the stock a bit more flavor.

Because the rice is toasted first, it takes less time to cook than in a standard paella. The liquid is added to very hot rice and tends to jump and sizzle, so add it carefully. Before pouring in the liquid, reduce the heat and let the rice and pan cool slightly.

As the name indicates, this Catalan dish traditionally uses Dublin Bay prawns *(escamarlans)*, but any prawn, or even colossal shrimp, will work. The dish is excellent accompanied by *Allioli* (page 81).

5 tablespoons extra-virgin olive oil

1 medium onion, roughly chopped

1 carrot, cut crosswise into 10 or so pieces

1 pound heads and bones of monkfish or another white fish

1 celery rib, cut into thirds

8 sprigs fresh flat-leaf parsley

8 peppercorns

1 teaspoon sweet *pimentón*

Salt

6 cups water

2 pinches saffron threads (about 20 total), lightly toasted and ground (see page 30)

12 to 16 raw head-on prawns (see page 34) or colossal shrimp with shells

2 garlic cloves, peeled

2 cups short- or medium-grain rice

Prepare the stock. In a Dutch oven or another medium heavy pot, heat 1 tablespoon of the oil over medium heat. Add the onion and carrot and cook for 5 minutes, stirring frequently, until they begin to brown and release their juices, about 5 minutes. Add the fish heads and bones, celery, parsley, peppercorns, *pimentón*, 2 pinches of salt, and water. Sprinkle

continued →

in the saffron. Bring to a simmer and continue simmering, partly covered, for 30 minutes. Strain the stock and set aside, discarding the solids.

In a 14- to 16-inch paella pan, heat the remaining 4 tablespoons of oil over medium heat. Add the prawns and garlic and cook until pale gold, watching very carefully that the garlic does not burn, about 5 minutes. Remove the garlic and discard. Transfer the prawns to a platter.

Remove any solids left in the oil with a skimmer or slotted spoon. Add the rice to the pan and cook, stirring constantly, until nutty brown and fragrant, about 10 minutes.

Meanwhile, in a clean medium saucepan, bring 5 cups of the broth to a boil.

Once the rice is browned, very carefully pour the hot stock into the paella over the rice. Taste for salt and adjust the seasoning as needed. With a wooden spoon, probe the pan to make sure the rice is evenly distributed. Do not stir again. Cook, uncovered, for 8 minutes over high heat. Lay the prawns atop the rice, reduce the heat to low, and cook for an additional 6 minutes, or until the liquid is absorbed and the rice is *al punto,* with just a bite to it.

Remove the paella from the heat, cover with paper towels, and let rest for 5 minutes before serving.

L'arròs fa el ventre

"Rice fills the gut and keeps the belly slim."

gros i la panxa llisa.

Rice Dishes from the **Cazuela** and **Caldero**

Arroz blanco con hierbas

White Rice with Herbs

SERVES 4 OR 6 AS A SIDE DISH | Montse Boschdemont is well known for her rice dishes in the tiny village of Canet d'Adri, outside Girona, Catalunya. Montse's mother-in-law opened the village shop-cum-café in the early part of the twentieth century, and then Montse ran it after her. It's closed now, except on special occasions, and Montse is mostly retired, though she still makes rices to go. They usually contain a mix of meat and seafood–rabbit, chicken, pork ribs, shellfish–and tend to be so moist they are almost runny. I have enjoyed these immensely over the last decade, but it is this simple, tasty white rice that I most associate with her. One late winter day, Montse taught me to make it in her kitchen, while five ducks with pears baked in the oven, dough for *bunyols* (fritters) rose, and a fire burned down in the fireplace opposite her wide stove.

This is the only rice dish in this cookbook that is served as an accompaniment, and it goes well with everything–meats, fresh sausages, fried eggs.

4½ cups water

2 garlic cloves, peeled

2 tablespoons chopped fresh flat-leaf parsley

1 tablespoon extra-virgin olive oil

Salt

2 cups short- or medium-grain rice

1 bay leaf

One 6-inch sprig fresh thyme, leaves and flowers stripped and discarded

In a large *cazuela* or a medium Dutch oven or another heavy pot, bring 4 cups of the water to a boil.

While the water heats, blend the garlic and parsley with the remaining ½ cup of water in a blender or food processor.

When the water in the *cazuela* reaches a boil, add the blended garlic-parsley mix, oil, and 1 pinch of salt. Stir and then add the rice, bay leaf, and stripped thyme stem. Cook, uncovered, stirring occasionally, for 10 minutes over medium-high heat and then check for salt, adjusting the seasoning as needed. Reduce the heat to low and cook for an additional 8 minutes, or until most of the liquid is absorbed and the rice is *al punto,* with just a bite to it.

Remove the *cazuela* from the heat, and transfer the rice to individual plates or a serving bowl. Let rest for a few minutes before serving.

Arroz de mar y montaña

"Sea and Mountain" Rice with Chicken, Pork Ribs, Shrimp, and Calamari

SERVES 6 | This dish is filled with the flavors of the sea and the mountains: pork, chicken, shrimp, and cuttlefish. The nutty, earthy flavors are punched up with a *picada* made with hazelnuts, which is even more intensely flavorful than one made with almonds. Watch the level of liquid and add more water if you want the rice more moist. The rice will look more brown than golden—perfect. It means there's lots of flavor.

1 pound pork spareribs, ribs cut apart and chopped into ¾-inch pieces

6 bone-in chicken thighs

Salt and freshly ground pepper

¼ cup extra-virgin olive oil

½ pound fresh pork sausage links, squeezed out of their casing into small balls (see Note)

12 to 18 large raw head-on shrimp with shells

1 pound cuttlefish or squid, cleaned and cut into 2-by-1-inch pieces (see page 35)

1 medium onion, finely chopped

4 ripe medium tomatoes, peeled, seeded, and finely chopped or coarsely grated (see page 23)

1 teaspoon sweet *pimentón*

7 cups water

2 garlic cloves, peeled

10 hazelnuts, without skins

1 teaspoon chopped fresh flat-leaf parsley

2 pinches saffron threads (about 20), lightly toasted and ground (see page 30)

2⅓ cups short- or medium-grain rice

Season the pork ribs and chicken generously with salt and pepper. In a large *cazuela* or medium Dutch oven or another heavy pot, heat the oil over medium heat. Cook the pork ribs and chicken, in 2 batches, until browned, about 5 to 7 minutes. Transfer to a large platter. In the same oil, add the sausages and shrimp and cook, turning the shrimp just once, about 4 minutes. Transfer to the platter.

Remove any solids left in the oil with a skimmer or slotted spoon and then prepare the *sofrito* in the same pan. Add the cuttlefish and cook for 2 minutes, stirring and scraping anything that sticks to the pan. Add the onion and cook, stirring frequently, until the cuttlefish has expelled its liquid and the onion is soft and nearly translucent, 5 to 10 minutes. Lower the heat to medium-low, add the tomatoes and 2 pinches of salt, and cook, stirring from time to time, until the tomato has darkened to a deeper shade of red and the *sofrito* is pasty, 10 to 15 minutes.

When the *sofrito* is ready, return the pork ribs, chicken, and sausages to the *cazuela*, along with any juices from the platter. Sprinkle in the *pimentón*, letting the flavors meld for a few seconds while stirring constantly. Add the water, bring to a simmer, and simmer, uncovered, for 30 minutes.

Meanwhile, prepare the *picada* by pounding in a mortar the garlic, hazelnuts, and parsley with 2 tablespoons of simmering liquid until you have a fine paste. Or whir them in a food processor or blender (see page 24).

Sprinkle the saffron into the *cazuela* and bring the liquid to a boil. Add the rice, stir in the *picada,* and return the shrimp to the pan. With a wooden spoon, probe the pan to make sure the rice is evenly distributed. Cook, uncovered, over medium-high heat for 10 minutes, occasionally stirring gently. Check for salt, adjusting the seasoning as needed. Reduce the heat to low and cook for an additional 8 minutes, or until the liquid is mostly absorbed and the rice is *al punto,* with just a bite to it.

Remove the *cazuela* from the heat and immediately transfer the food to plates, letting the rice rest for a few minutes before serving.

NOTE: *Look for breakfast links that are unsweetened or Italian sausages that are not spiced or flavored. To remove the sausage from its casing, hold a link with one hand while pinching and pulling out pieces the size of marbles with the other, sliding them down the casing and out the end.*

Arroz de bacalao y verdures

Rice with Salt Cod and Vegetables

SERVES 6 | Any recipe that begins with "Two days before" is one that I usually skip. But while this recipe needs to be started ahead, so the salt cod can be slowly desalinated, there is little to do in those two days but change the water a few times.

Spanish, Italian, and Portuguese markets often sell different cuts of salt cod. The center-cut *lomo* is expensive but is also the meatiest and takes the least work to prepare. After the salt cod has been soaked, it needs to be carefully deboned. Needle-nose pliers work well for stubborn bones, which you are most likely to encounter in the less expensive cuts.

1 pound salt cod

¼ cup extra-virgin olive oil

1 medium onion, roughly chopped

½ red bell pepper, cored, seeded, and cut into ½-square-inch pieces

½ green bell pepper, cored, seeded, and cut into ½-square-inch pieces

3 medium artichokes, trimmed, tough parts of leaves removed, cut into eighths, and choke scraped out

2 garlic cloves, finely chopped

4 ripe medium tomatoes, peeled, seeded, and finely chopped or coarsely grated (see page 23)

Salt

½ teaspoon sweet *pimentón*

2 pinches saffron threads (about 20), lightly toasted and ground (see page 30)

7 cups Fish Stock (page 26)

3 cups short- or medium-grain rice

6 spears fresh green asparagus, bottoms trimmed, and cut into 1-inch pieces

Two days before you plan to serve, put the salt cod in a large bowl and cover with fresh water. Change the water immediately, rinse out the bowl, and refill with cool water. Let the cod soak for 24 hours. Then change the water every 8 hours or so for the next 24 hours. Drain the cod, rinse, and gently squeeze out some of the excess water. Skin and carefully debone. Shred into bite-size pieces.

Prepare the *sofrito*. In a large *cazuela* or medium Dutch oven or another heavy pot, heat the oil over medium heat. Add the onion, bell peppers, and artichokes and cook until the onion is soft and nearly translucent and the artichokes and peppers begin to brown, about 10 minutes. Lower the heat to medium-low, add the garlic, tomatoes, and 2 pinches of salt and cook, continuing to stir from time to time, until the tomato has darkened to a deeper shade of red and the *sofrito* is pasty, 10 to 15 minutes.

When the *sofrito* is ready, sprinkle the *pimentón* and saffron into the *cazuela*, letting the flavors meld for a few seconds while stirring constantly. Add the stock and bring to a boil. Add the rice and pieces of cod. With a wooden spoon, probe the pan to make sure the rice is evenly distributed. Cook, uncovered, over medium-high heat for 10 minutes, gently stirring occasionally. Check for salt, adjusting the seasoning as needed. Add the asparagus, reduce the heat to low, and cook for an additional 8 minutes, or until most of the liquid is absorbed and the rice is *al punto,* with just a bite to it.

Remove the *cazuela* from the heat and immediately transfer the food to plates, letting the rice rest for a few minutes before serving.

Arroz con sardinas

Rice with Sardines

SERVES 6 | The humble sardine can be sublime, as this dish demonstrates. It's best when the fish are running. In Spain their peak falls *de Virgen a Virgen* ("from Virgin to Virgin"), that is, between the feast days of Carmen (July 16) and the Assumption of the Virgin Mary into Heaven (August 15). I prefer small sardines, about 4 inches long and weighing a little under 1 ounce each. I leave them whole, pick them off the rice, and eat them with my fingers. This dish is started on the stove top. When the rice is half cooked, the sardines are laid on top decoratively like spokes of a wheel, and the *cazuela* is slid into the oven for 10 minutes.

¼ cup extra-virgin olive oil

1 medium onion, finely chopped

2 cloves garlic, finely chopped

3 ripe medium tomatoes, peeled, seeded, and finely chopped or coarsely grated (see page 23)

Salt

½ teaspoon sweet *pimentón*

2 pinches saffron threads (about 20), lightly toasted and ground (see page 30)

6½ cups Fish Stock (page 26)

3 cups short- or medium-grain rice

¾ cup fresh or thawed frozen peas

12 to 18 fresh sardines (about 1 to 1½ pounds total, see Note)

Make the *sofrito*. In a large *cazuela* or medium Dutch oven or another heavy pot, heat the oil over medium-low heat. Add the onion and cook until soft and nearly translucent, 5 to 10 minutes. Add the garlic, tomatoes, and 2 pinches of salt and cook, stirring from time to time, until the tomato has darkened to a deeper shade of red and the *sofrito* is pasty, 10 to 15 minutes.

Preheat oven to 400°F.

When the *sofrito* is ready, sprinkle in the *pimentón* and saffron, letting the flavors meld for a few seconds while stirring constantly. Add the stock, increase the heat, and bring to a boil. Add the rice and peas. With a wooden spoon, probe the pan to make sure the rice is evenly distributed. Check for salt, adjusting the seasoning as needed. Cook, uncovered, over

continued →

medium-high heat for 10 minutes, gently stirring occasionally. Remove from the heat.

Working quickly, lay the sardines across the top of the rice like spokes on a wheel, cover loosely with aluminum foil, and place in the hot oven. Bake until most of the liquid is absorbed (it doesn't need to be dry), the rice is *al punto,* with just a bite to it, and the eyes of the sardines are cloudy, about 10 minutes.

Remove the *cazuela* from the oven and immediately transfer the food to plates, letting the rice rest for a few minutes before serving.

NOTE: *While smaller sardines weighing around 1 ounce each are laid whole on the rice, larger sardines should be cleaned and butterflied open, with the heads and spines removed. Or you can fillet them. The cooking time remains the same.*

Arroz de rape, gambas, y almejas
Rice with Monkfish, Shrimp, and Clams

SERVES 4 | We like this *cazuela* rice dish very moist, almost *caldoso,* and use plenty of liquid. The nutty *picada* complements the flavors of the seafood nicely. Be sure to pound it finely so that there are not crunchy pieces of almond left. The *picada* should be evident only by the flavorful undertone that it lends the dish.

20 small clams (about 6 ounces), purged of sand (see Note, page 47)

Salt

1 garlic clove, peeled

6 whole almonds, toasted (see Note, page 66)

1 teaspoon chopped fresh flat-leaf parsley

1 pound monkfish steaks

Freshly ground pepper

¼ cup extra-virgin olive oil

Flour for dredging

12 jumbo raw head-on shrimp with shells

1 medium onion, finely chopped

½ red bell pepper, cored, seeded, and cut into ½-inch-square pieces

4 ripe medium tomatoes, peeled, seeded, and finely chopped or coarsely grated (see page 23)

1 teaspoon sweet *pimentón*

1 pinch saffron threads (about 10), lightly toasted and ground (see page 30)

5½ cups Fish Stock (page 26) or a quick shrimp stock (see Note, page 104)

1½ cups short- or medium-grain rice

In a small saucepan, bring a few cups of water to a boil and add the clams and a pinch of salt. Reduce the heat and simmer, partly covered, until the clams have opened, 5 to 10 minutes. Remove from the heat and set aside, covered, leaving the clams in the water. (Discard any that do not open.)

Meanwhile, prepare the *picada* by pounding in a mortar the garlic, almonds, and parsley with 2 tablespoons of stock until you have a fine paste. Or whir them in a food processor or blender (see page 24).

Season the fish steaks generously with salt and pepper. In a large *cazuela* or medium

continued →

Dutch oven or another heavy pot, heat the oil over medium heat. When the oil begins to shimmer, dredge the fish, piece by piece, in the flour and then cook, turning just once, until golden, 1 to 2 minutes per side. Transfer to a platter. In the same pan, cook the shrimp until pink, about 2 minutes on each side. Transfer to the platter.

Remove any solids left in the oil with a skimmer or slotted spoon and prepare the *sofrito* in the same pan. Reduce the heat to medium-low, add the onion, and cook, stirring frequently, until soft and nearly translucent, 5 to 10 minutes. Add the bell pepper and cook for 5 minutes more. Add the tomatoes and 2 pinches of salt and cook, stirring from time to time, until the tomato has darkened to a deeper shade of red and the *sofrito* is pasty, 10 to 15 minutes.

Drain the clams. Discard one shell (the empty one) from each clam.

When the *sofrito* is ready, sprinkle the *pimentón* and saffron into the *cazuela*, letting the flavors meld for a few seconds while stirring constantly. Add the stock and bring to a boil. Add the rice and clams and spoon in the *picada*. Cook, uncovered, over medium-high heat for 10 minutes, gently stirring occasionally. Check for salt, adjusting the seasoning as needed. Return the shrimp and monkfish to the *cazuela*, reduce the heat to low, and cook for an additional 8 minutes, or until most of the liquid is absorbed and the rice is *al punto,* with just a bite to it.

Remove the *cazuela* from the heat and immediately transfer the food to plates, letting the rice rest for a few minutes before serving.

NOTE: *To make a quick shrimp stock, remove the heads of the shrimp after frying, combine the heads with 1 cup of water in a blender, and purée for 20 seconds. Pour into a deep saucepan and add another 5 cups of water, ½ onion, 12 peppercorns, and 2 pinches of salt. Bring to a boil, reduce the heat, and simmer for 30 minutes. Strain through a fine-mesh chinois, discarding any solids. The yield is 5½ cups, perfect for this recipe.*

Arroz de pollo

Rice with Chicken

SERVES 6 | Rice dishes often draw on various, sometimes disparate, flavors. Not this one. This is rice cooked with chicken. No seafood, rabbit, or pork. No artichokes or wild mushrooms. Just chicken. And though seafood, rabbit, or pork would make lovely additions, sometimes one wants just chicken. And this dish draws out its flavor to the fullest. To make it richer and denser, drop a small handful of toasted almonds or hazelnuts into the *picada*.

1 whole free-range organic chicken (about 3 pounds)

4 tablespoons extra-virgin olive oil

1½ medium onions, finely chopped

1 carrot, cut in half

1 celery rib

8 to 12 sprigs fresh flat-leaf parsley, leaves stripped, and stems and
   leaves reserved separately

1 bay leaf

8 peppercorns

Salt

9½ cups water

Freshly ground pepper

4 ripe medium tomatoes, peeled, seeded, and finely chopped or coarsely
   grated (see page 23)

1 garlic clove, peeled

½ teaspoon sweet *pimentón*

2 pinches saffron threads (about 20), lightly toasted and ground (see
   page 30)

3 cups short- or medium-grain rice

Disjoint the chicken, reserving the back and neck. Trim off some of the fat, but leave the skin intact. Chop the chicken with a cleaver into 12 to 24 small pieces. Carefully pick out any bone shards.

In a stockpot, Dutch oven, or another large heavy pot, heat 1 tablespoon of oil over medium heat. Add the back, neck, one third of the onion, and the carrot and cook until they begin to brown, about 5 minutes. Reduce the heat to low and cook for another 5 minutes, until they release their juices. Add the celery, parsley stems, bay leaf, peppercorns, 2 pinches of salt, and the water. Bring to a boil, reduce the heat, and simmer, covered, for 45 minutes. Strain and reserve the liquid, discarding the solids.

While the stock is simmering, season the chicken generously with salt and pepper. In a large *cazuela* or medium Dutch oven or another heavy pot, heat the remaining 3 tablespoons of oil over medium heat. Add the chicken and cook until browned, about 5 minutes. Transfer to a large platter.

Prepare the *sofrito* in the same pan. Reduce the heat to medium-low, add the remaining onion, and cook, stirring frequently, until softened and nearly translucent, 5 to 10 minutes. Add the tomatoes and 2 pinches of salt and cook, stirring from time to time, until the tomato has darkened to a deeper shade of red and the *sofrito* is pasty, 10 to 15 minutes.

Return the chicken to the *cazuela* along with any juices from the platter, add 1 cup of liquid from the stockpot, and let simmer slowly over low heat for 15 minutes, or until the stock is ready.

Meanwhile, prepare the *picada* by pounding in a mortar the garlic and parsley leaves with 2 tablespoons of stock until you have a fine paste. Or whir them in a food processor or blender (see page 24).

Sprinkle the *pimentón* and saffron into the *cazuela,* letting the flavors meld for a few seconds while stirring constantly. Add the remaining 8 cups of stock, increase the heat, and bring to a boil. Add the rice and spoon in the *picada.* With a wooden spoon, probe the pan to make sure the rice is evenly distributed. Cook, uncovered, over medium-high heat for 10 minutes, gently stirring occasionally. Check for salt, adjusting the seasoning as needed. Reduce the heat to low and cook for an additional 8 minutes, or until most of the liquid is absorbed and the rice is *al punto,* with just a bite to it.

Remove the *cazuela* from the heat and immediately transfer the food to plates, letting the rice rest for a few minutes before serving.

Arroz de cazadores

Hunter's Rice with Rabbit and Quail

SERVES 6 | This meaty rice captures the flavors of the countryside. The liver is pounded into the *picada* to give the dish more intense tones of the forest. Some aromatics—a sprig of fresh rosemary, a bay leaf, the stripped sprig of thyme—or a handful of wild mushrooms are perfect here, too, and can be added when the meats are stewing.

1 whole rabbit (about 2½ pounds), cut into about 12 pieces, liver reserved

3 whole quail, cleaned and quartered

Salt and freshly ground pepper

¼ cup extra-virgin olive oil

1 medium onion, finely chopped

¼ pound green beans, ends trimmed, and cut into 1- to 2-inch pieces

1 carrot, cut into thin rounds

4 ripe medium tomatoes, peeled, seeded, and finely chopped or coarsely grated (see page 23)

1 teaspoon sweet *pimentón*

8 cups water

2 garlic cloves, peeled

12 whole almonds, toasted (see Note, page 66)

1 tablespoon chopped fresh flat-leaf parsley

2 pinches saffron threads (about 20), lightly toasted and ground (see page 30)

2½ cups short- or medium-grain rice

Season the rabbit and quail generously with salt and pepper. In a large *cazuela* or medium Dutch oven or another heavy pot, heat the oil over medium heat. In 2 batches, cook the rabbit, rabbit liver, and quail until browned and the liver is cooked through, 5 to 7 minutes for each batch. Transfer to a large platter.

Prepare the *sofrito* in the same pan. Reduce heat to medium-low, add the onion,

and cook, stirring frequently, until soft and nearly translucent, 5 to 10 minutes. Add the green beans and carrot and cook for 5 minutes more. Add the tomatoes and 2 pinches of salt and cook, stirring from time to time, until the tomato has darkened to a deeper shade of red and the *sofrito* is pasty, 10 to 15 minutes.

Return the rabbit and quail to the *cazuela* along with any juices from the platter. Sprinkle in the *pimentón,* letting the flavors meld for a few seconds while stirring constantly. Add the water, bring to a simmer, and continue simmering, uncovered, for 30 minutes.

Meanwhile, prepare the *picada* by pounding in a mortar the reserved liver, garlic, almonds, and parsley with 2 tablespoons of the simmering liquid until you have a fine paste. Or whir them in a food processor or blender (see page 24).

Sprinkle in the saffron and bring the liquid in the *cazuela* to a boil. Add the rice and stir in the *picada.* Cook, uncovered, over medium-high heat for 10 minutes, gently stirring occasionally. Check for salt, adjusting the seasoning as needed. Reduce the heat to low and cook for an additional 8 minutes, or until most of the liquid is absorbed and the rice is *al punto,* with just a bite to it.

Remove the *cazuela* from the heat and immediately transfer the food to plates, letting the rice rest for a few minutes before serving.

Arroz de pichón y setas

Rice with Squab and Wild Mushrooms

SERVES 6 | I like this dish with tender squab (a young domesticated pigeon that has never flown, usually about four weeks old), but it is also excellent with quail or partridge. Poussin (a small, young chicken) can be used as well, and even Cornish game hen. For quail and poussin figure one per person; for partridge and game hen, figure one bird per two people. Buy the freshest-looking wild mushrooms in the market, preferably two or three different kinds. If you can't find wild ones, classic cultivated white mushrooms will work fine.

6 squab or quail, or 3 partridges, cleaned and quartered

Salt and freshly ground pepper

4 tablespoons extra-virgin olive oil

4 slices thickly cut bacon, cut into 1½-inch-long pieces

2 garlic cloves, peeled

1 medium onion, chopped

4 ripe medium tomatoes, peeled, seeded, and finely chopped or coarsely grated (see page 23)

10 whole almonds, toasted (see Note, page 66)

1 tablespoon chopped fresh flat-leaf parsley

8 cups Chicken Stock (page 28)

1 teaspoon sweet *pimentón*

¾ pound assorted wild mushrooms, cleaned (see page 34) and cut into pieces

2 pinches saffron threads (about 20), lightly toasted and ground (see page 30)

3 cups short- or medium-grain rice

Season the squab generously with salt and pepper. In a large *cazuela* or medium Dutch oven or another heavy pot, heat 2 tablespoons of the oil over medium heat. Add the bacon and garlic and cook until golden (be careful not to burn the garlic), about 5 minutes. Transfer both to a platter. Add the squab to the pan and cook, stirring frequently, until golden, about 5 minutes. Transfer to the platter.

Remove any solids left in the oil with a skimmer or slotted spoon and prepare the *sofrito* in the same *cazuela*. Add the onion and

continued →

cook over medium-low heat until soft and nearly translucent, 5 to 10 minutes. Add the tomatoes and 2 pinches of salt and cook, stirring from time to time, until the tomato has darkened to a deeper shade of red and the *sofrito* is pasty, 10 to 15 minutes.

Meanwhile, prepare the *picada* by pounding in a mortar the sautéed garlic and the almonds and parsley with 2 tablespoons of stock until you have a fine paste. Or whir them in a food processor or blender (see page 24).

When the *sofrito* is ready, sprinkle the *pimentón* into the *cazuela,* letting the flavors meld for some seconds while stirring constantly. Return the bacon and squab to the *cazuela* along with any juices from the platter, add 1 cup of stock, and simmer over low heat until the liquid has evaporated.

While this mixture simmers, prepare the mushrooms. Heat the remaining 2 tablespoons of oil in a large sauté pan over medium-low heat. Add the mushrooms and 2 pinches of salt and cook slowly until the mushrooms begin to brown and have expelled their liquid, about 5 minutes. Drain and reserve the liquid. Increase the heat to high and cook the mushrooms for another 2 minutes. Transfer to the platter.

Add the remaining 7 cups of stock and the reserved mushroom broth to the *cazuela,* sprinkle in the saffron, increase the heat, and bring to a boil. Add the rice and spoon in the *picada.* Cook, uncovered, over medium-high heat for 10 minutes, gently stirring occasion-

ally. Check for salt, adjusting the seasoning as needed. Distribute the mushrooms evenly around the pan. Reduce the heat to low and cook for an additional 8 minutes, or until most of the liquid is absorbed and the rice is *al punto,* with just a bite to it.

Remove the *cazuela* from the heat and immediately transfer the food to plates, letting the rice rest for a few minutes before serving.

112

Arroz caldoso de verduras y almejas

Soupy Rice with Vegetables and Clams

SERVES 4 | When my wife, Eva, was growing up, her mother prepared this soupy rice often. It was also the first thing Eva cooked for me. That was more than a decade ago, in the cramped kitchen of our student residence hall in London, and I remember the meal well. It can be cooked with just vegetables, but the clams—and the broth from cooking them—give the flavors a boost. *Caldoso* comes from *caldo,* stock, and this dish should have some in every spoonful.

7 cups water

¾ pound small or medium clams, purged of sand (see Note, page 47)

Salt

½ garlic clove, peeled

1½ teaspoons chopped fresh flat-leaf parsley

2 tablespoons extra-virgin olive oil

½ medium onion, roughly chopped

½ carrot, cut into thin discs

¼ pound leeks (white and green parts), cut into ½- to 1-inch pieces

½ green bell pepper, cored, seeded, and cut into ½-inch-dice

¼ pound green beans, ends trimmed and cut into 1-inch pieces

½ teaspoon sweet *pimentón*

2 pinches saffron threads (about 20), lightly toasted and ground (see page 30)

1½ cups short- or medium-grain rice

In a medium saucepan, bring the water to a boil and add the clams and a pinch of salt. Reduce the heat and simmer, partly covered, for 30 minutes. Remove from the heat and set aside, covered, leaving the clams in the water. (Discard any that do not open.)

Meanwhile, prepare the *picada* by pounding in a mortar the garlic and parsley with 1 tablespoon of the simmering liquid until you have a fine paste. Or whir them in a food processor or blender (see page 24).

In a *caldero,* tall *cazuela,* medium Dutch oven, or another heavy pot, heat 2 tablespoons of the oil over medium-low heat. Add the onion, carrot, and leek, and cook, stirring frequently, until they begin to brown and release their

continued →

juices, about 5 minutes. Add the bell pepper and green beans and cook for another 5 minutes, until softened.

Meanwhile, strain the broth from the clams and reserve it. Discard one shell (the empty one) from each clam, and set aside the rest.

When the vegetables are softened, sprinkle the *pimentón* and saffron into the *cazuela,* letting the flavors meld for a few seconds while stirring constantly. Add 6½ cups of the clam broth, increase the heat, and bring to a boil. Add the rice, spoon in the *picada,* and add the clams. Cook, uncovered, over medium-high heat for 10 minutes, gently stirring occasionally. Check for salt, adjusting the seasoning as needed. Reduce the heat to low and cook for an additional 8 minutes, or until the rice is *al punto,* with just a bite to it.

Ladle the *caldoso* rice into bowls and serve immediately.

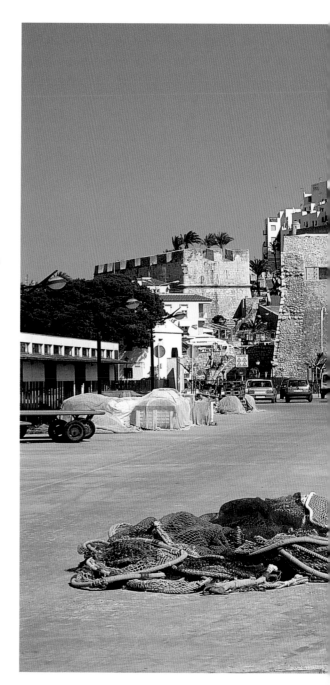

Arroz caldoso de pato y rebozuelos
Soupy Rice with Duck and Chanterelles

SERVES 6 | This slowly stewed rice dish is one of our cold-weather favorites. Use whichever wild mushroom you can find—chanterelles, morels, cèpes. Along with chanterelles, my favorite mushrooms to use in this dish are *camagrocs* (in Catalan, literally, "yellow legs"; *Cantharellus lutescens*), a trumpet-shaped, apricot-colored mushroom that grows in Spain from fall into late winter. They're flavorful and fragrant, and stand up well in the pot.

Sauté the mushrooms over medium-low heat so that while they cook, their flavorful liquid is expelled without instantly evaporating. That liquid is added to the rice. For an earthier flavor, add the duck liver to the *picada*.

1 duck (about 3½ pounds), liver reserved (optional)

Salt and freshly ground pepper

5 tablespoons extra-virgin olive oil

1 medium onion, finely chopped

4 ripe medium tomatoes, peeled, seeded, and finely chopped or coarsely
grated (see page 23)

1 teaspoon sweet *pimentón*

9 cups water

One 6-inch sprig of thyme, leaves and flowers stripped and discarded

One 6-inch sprig of rosemary, needles stripped and discarded

1 bay leaf

10 ounces fresh chanterelles, *camagrocs,* morels, cèpes, or other wild
mushrooms, cleaned (see page 34) and cut into pieces if larger than
2 inches

2 garlic cloves, peeled

10 whole almonds, toasted (see Note, page 66)

1 teaspoon chopped fresh flat-leaf parsley

2 pinches saffron threads (about 20), lightly toasted and ground (see
page 30)

2 cups short- or medium-grain rice

Remove most of the skin and fat from the duck, and trim off the neck, the feet, and wing tips at the first joint. Disjoint the duck. Rinse well with fresh water and pat dry with paper towels. Prick the remaining skin with a fork to help render the fat when the duck cooks. Season generously with salt and pepper.

In a *caldero,* tall *cazuela,* medium Dutch oven, or another heavy pot, heat 3 tablespoons of oil over medium heat. Cook the duck (and liver, if using) in 2 batches if necessary, until browned and the fat has been rendered, about 5 minutes. Transfer to a large platter. Remove all but a thin coating of fat from the pan.

Begin making the *sofrito* in the same pan. Add the onion, and slowly cook over medium-low heat until soft and translucent, 5 to 10 minutes. Add the tomatoes and 2 pinches of salt and cook, stirring from time to time, until the tomato has darkened to a deeper shade of red and the *sofrito* is pasty, 10 to 15 minutes.

When the *sofrito* is ready, sprinkle in the *pimentón,* letting the flavors meld for a few seconds while stirring constantly. Return the duck to the pan, turning the pieces around the pan for 1 minute to absorb the flavors. Add the water, stripped thyme and rosemary stems, and bay leaf, increase the heat, and bring to a boil. Reduce the heat to low and simmer, covered, for 1½ hours.

Meanwhile, heat the remaining 2 tablespoons of oil in a large sauté pan over medium-low heat. Cook the mushrooms, garlic, and 2 pinches of salt, stirring occasionally, until the mushrooms have expelled their liquid, about 5 minutes. Drain and reserve the liquid.

Increase the heat to high, and cook the mushrooms and garlic for another 2 minutes. Transfer to a platter.

Prepare the *picada* by pounding in a mortar the reserved liver, garlic, almonds, and parsley with 2 tablespoons of the simmering liquid until you have a fine paste. Or whir them in a food processor or blender (see page 24).

Remove the herb stems and bay leaf from the *cazuela* and discard. Transfer the pieces of duck to a platter. As soon as the duck can be handled, pull the meat off the bones, discarding the bones and the fat. Return the meat along with any juices from the platter to the pot.

Sprinkle in the saffron and spoon in the *picada.* Increase the heat, and when the liquid is at a boil, add the rice. Cook, uncovered, over medium-high heat for 10 minutes, gently stirring occasionally. Check for salt, adjusting the seasoning as needed. Add the mushrooms and their expelled liquid. Reduce the heat to low and cook for an additional 8 minutes, or until the rice is *al punto,* with just a bite to it.

Remove the *caldoso* rice from the heat, cover with a lid, and bring to the table. Lift the lid, allowing all to smell the aromas wafting out of the pot, and ladle into bowls immediately.

Arroz caldoso de bogavante
Soupy Rice with Lobster

SERVES 4 | The *bogavante* we cook in Spain is a European lobster, a close cousin to its American counterpart. I like to use 2 lobsters that weigh about 1 pound each, though a single, larger one can be used.

A *picada* changes the flavor, color, and even the texture of the rice. Here, along with the traditional garlic, almonds, and parsley, the *picada* has *ñora* peppers. These small, round, dried sweet red peppers add a robust flavor and are worth seeking out. They need to be soaked in water and softened, and then lightly fried in oil before they are pounded into the *picada*.

2 small *ñora* peppers or 1 ancho chile

Two 1-pound live lobsters

Salt and freshly ground pepper

4 tablespoons extra-virgin olive oil

1 medium onion, ½ roughly chopped, and ½ finely chopped

1 carrot, cut crosswise into 10 or so pieces

2 pounds heads and bones of monkfish or another white fish

1 celery rib, cut crosswise into thirds

8 sprigs fresh flat-leaf parsley, leaves stripped and stems and leaves
    reserved separately

8 peppercorns

7 cups water

2 garlic cloves, peeled

1 squid (about 2 ounces), cleaned and cut into ½-inch square pieces

¼ green bell pepper, cored, seeded, and cut into ½-inch square pieces

2 ripe medium tomatoes, peeled, seeded, and finely chopped or coarsely
    grated (see page 23)

6 whole almonds, toasted (see Note, page 66)

1 teaspoon chopped fresh flat-leaf parsley

½ teaspoon sweet *pimentón*

2 pinches saffron threads (about 20), lightly toasted and ground (see
    page 30)

1½ cups short- or medium-grain rice

continued →

Soak the *ñoras* in a small bowl of warm water for 1 hour. Drain, and remove and discard the stem and seeds. Chop the flesh and set aside.

With a very sharp knife, split the lobsters in half lengthwise, cutting along the belly and catching any juice that falls. Season generously with salt and pepper. In a stockpot or medium Dutch oven or another heavy pot, heat 2 tablespoons of the oil over medium heat. Add the lobsters and cook for 2 minutes, meat-side down, then for another 2 minutes shell-side down. Transfer to a platter.

In the same pot, add the roughly chopped onion and the carrot and cook, stirring frequently, until they begin to brown and release their juices, about 5 minutes. Add the fish heads and bones, celery, parsley stems, peppercorns, and 2 pinches of salt, and cover with the water. Cut away the lobster appendages and the head. Transfer the body and large claws to the platter and add the rest to the stock. Bring to a boil, reduce the heat, and cook, partly covered, for 30 minutes. Strain the stock, discarding the solids.

While the stock is simmering, begin making the *sofrito*. In a *caldero,* tall *cazuela,* medium Dutch oven, or another heavy medium pot, heat 2 tablespoons of oil over medium-low heat. Cook the pieces of *ñora* peppers and the garlic until the garlic is brown, about 5 minutes, watching the garlic carefully so that it does not burn. Transfer to a platter. Add the remaining onion and slowly cook until soft and translucent, 5 to 10 minutes. Add the squid and bell pepper, and cook for another 5 minutes. Add the tomatoes and 2 pinches of salt, and cook, stirring from time to time, until the tomato has darkened to a deeper shade of red and the *sofrito* is pasty, 10 to 15 minutes.

Next, prepare the *picada* by pounding in a mortar the *ñoras,* garlic, almonds, and parsley with 2 tablespoons of stock until you have a fine paste. Or whir them in a food processor or blender (see page 24).

Cut the lobster bodies into half-moon-shaped pieces, keeping the meat attached to the shell if possible. Pick out any tiny shards of shell and discard. Gently crack the large claws so they remain intact but the meat is very accessible.

When the *sofrito* is ready, sprinkle in the *pimentón* and saffron, letting the flavors meld for a few seconds while stirring constantly. Add 6½ cups of the stock and spoon in the *picada*. Increase the heat and when the liquid is at a boil, add the rice and the pieces of lobster along with any juices from the platter. Cook, uncovered, over medium-high heat for 10 minutes, gently stirring occasionally. Check for salt, adjusting the seasoning as needed. Reduce the heat to low and cook for an additional 8 minutes, or until the rice is *al punto,* with just a bite to it.

Remove the *caldoso* rice from the heat, cover with a lid, and bring to the table. Lift the lid, allowing all to smell the aromas floating out of the pot, and ladle into bowls immediately.

Caldero de arroz de pescado de roca y tallarines de sepia

Caldron of Soupy Rice with Rockfish and Strips of Cuttlefish

SERVES 4 | La Vinya del Senyor is a wine bar not far from my Barcelona flat. It specializes in wine, of course, but it also serves a handful of dishes that are, without fail, original and delicious. The cook there is the young Ismael Prados. He has one of the most recognized faces in all of Catalunya because of his daily TV cooking program and the covers of his best-selling cookbooks. Yet very few people know he works the stoves at La Vinya del Senyor at night. I have adapted this recipe, which he serves at the bar, only slightly. I love the anise in the *picada,* the long thin slices of cuttlefish, and the sautéed and roasted shore crabs for the stock. When I want to wow friends at our table, I often prepare this rice.

1 medium cuttlefish tube or 2 squid tubes (see page 35)

ROCKFISH STOCK

2 tablespoons extra-virgin olive oil

1 onion, diced

1 leek (white and green parts), diced

1 small carrot, diced

1 celery rib, diced

½ teaspoon sweet *pimentón*

1 ripe large tomato, peeled, seeded, and finely chopped or coarsely grated (see page 23)

8 cups water

½ pound live small crabs (see Note, page 126)

2 tablespoons sunflower oil

2½ pounds assorted rockfish

6 sprigs fresh flat-leaf parsley or cilantro

5 tablespoons extra-virgin olive oil

1 clove garlic, peeled

1 onion, finely chopped

4 ripe large plum tomatoes, peeled, seeded, and finely chopped or
    coarsely grated (see page 23)
Salt
4 whole almonds, toasted (see Note, page 66)
4 whole hazelnuts, without skins
12 leaves fresh flat-leaf parsley
10 anise seeds
10 saffron threads, lightly toasted (see page 30)
1½ cups short-grain Bomba rice
Freshly ground pepper

Cut the cuttlefish tube open and flatten. Wrap in plastic wrap so it remains flat, place in the freezer, and freeze until firm, about 1 hour. Remove the plastic and cut the tube with a sharp knife into long, very thin, tagliatelle-like strips. (Slightly wider but as flat as fettuccine.) Reserve in the refrigerator until ready to use.

Preheat the oven to 400°F.

Prepare the rockfish stock. In a stockpot or medium Dutch oven or another heavy pot, heat the oil over medium-high heat. Add the onion and cook until golden, about 3 minutes. Reduce the heat to medium-low and add the leek. Cook, letting it sweat its moisture for 2 to 3 minutes. Add the carrot and celery and cook until wilted, about 5 minutes. Sprinkle in the *pimentón* and cook, stirring constantly, for 10 seconds, until it has darkened the vegetables. Add the tomato and cook, stirring occasionally, until it has darkened and lost its acidity, 5 to 10 minutes. Pour in the water and bring to a simmer.

Kill the crabs by crushing them with a wooden mallet. Heat the sunflower oil in a large skillet over high heat. Add the crabs and quickly sauté until the shells are red, about 2 minutes. Transfer with a slotted spoon to a baking pan and immediately put into the hot oven. Roast the crabs for 10 minutes.

Add the roasted crabs to the simmering stock, and simmer for 5 minutes. Add the rockfish and simmer, uncovered, for 20 minutes. Remove from the heat and add the parsley. Let the parsley infuse the stock as it cools down.

While the stock cools, prepare the *sofrito*. In a tall *cazuela*, medium Dutch oven, or another medium heavy pot, heat 3 tablespoons of the olive oil over medium-low heat. Add the garlic and cook until pale gold. Transfer to a plate. Add the onion and slowly cook until soft and translucent, 5 to 10 minutes. Add the tomatoes and 2 pinches of salt and cook, stirring from time to time, until the tomato has darkened to a deeper shade of red and the *sofrito* is pasty, 10 to 15 minutes.

Meanwhile, prepare the *picada* by pounding in a mortar the garlic, almonds, hazelnuts, parsley, anise, and saffron with 2 tablespoons of stock until you have a fine paste. Or whir them in a food processor or blender (see page 24).

125

continued →

Caldero de arroz de pescado de roca
y tallarines de sepia
(continued)

Strain the fish stock, discarding the solids. In a medium saucepan bring 6 cups of the stock to a boil.

When the *sofrito* is ready, add the rice, letting the flavors meld for 1 minute while stirring constantly. Increase the heat to medium-high and pour in the boiling stock. Taste for salt and adjust the seasoning as needed.

Meanwhile, season the cuttlefish with salt and pepper. After the rice has cooked for 8 minutes, heat the remaining 2 tablespoons of olive oil in a sauté pan over medium heat. Add the cuttlefish and quickly sauté until golden, about 4 minutes. Add to the rice.

When the rice is almost *al punto,* after 12 to 14 minutes of cooking, stir in the *picada.*

Remove from the heat, cover with a lid, and bring to the table. Lift the lid, allowing all to smell the aromas that float out, and ladle into bowls immediately.

NOTE: *Small crabs, about 2 to 3 inches across the shell, are a favorite addition to the soup and stockpots here. Any small crab, preferably no larger than 3½ inches across the shell, will work, including shore crabs, shamefaced crabs, or swimming crabs. Look for these in well-stocked fish and seafood markets or Asian grocery stores.*

No hay boda sin arroz,

"There is no wedding without rice, nor youngster without love."

ni mocita sin amor.

Rice Desserts

Arroz con leche

Rice Pudding

SERVES 4 | There are few smells more inviting than that of rice simmering in milk with sugar, cinnamon, and citrus peels. We like to make *arroz con leche* on fall or winter weekend mornings, when the doors and windows of our Barcelona flat are snugly closed, and there is little impetus to rush out, perhaps only for the newspaper and mid-morning pastry. The recipe we like is traditional and contains just a few ingredients, including both lemon and orange peels. (Many, including my mother-in-law, use only lemon peels, but I prefer the slightly sweeter tang that orange brings.) It's a creamy dessert, sweet, with slightly chewy rice and hints of Spain's Moorish legacy.

⅔ cup short- or medium-grain rice

4 cups whole milk

1 stick cinnamon

Peel of ½ orange, the white pith scraped away

Peel of ½ lemon, the white pith scraped away

⅔ cup sugar

Ground cinnamon for dusting (optional)

Put the rice in a 2-quart saucepan and barely cover with cold water. Bring to a brisk boil over high heat, and then immediately remove from the heat. Drain the rice in a colander, but do not rinse. Set aside.

In the same saucepan, over medium-high heat, bring the milk to a boil with the cinnamon and citrus peels. Once bubbles break the surface, return the rice to the pan and then add the sugar, stirring to break up any clumps of rice and dissolve the sugar. Reduce the heat and simmer, partly covered, for about 40 minutes, or until most of the milk is absorbed and the rice is still chewy. Stir occasionally to prevent the rice from burning or clumping, and to prevent a thick skin from forming on the surface.

Have 4 flan or dessert cups ready.

Discard the cinnamon stick and citrus peels. Divide the pudding among the bowls with a ladle. Let cool and then refrigerate for at least 1 hour. If desired, dust the surface of each with ground cinnamon immediately before serving.

Menjar blanc

Rice Flour and Almond Pudding

SERVES 4 | The name of this ancient dessert means "white food." The fourteenth century Catalan cookery book *Llibre de Sent Soví* gives a recipe for *menjar blanc* made with rice, chicken, sugar, almonds, and rosewater. These days, it is made as a thick rice flour and almond pudding (without the chicken), and is best known in the Tarragona city of Reus. In some modern versions, starch is substituted for rice flour.

3½ ounces raw almonds, finely ground, plus ¼ cup slivered almonds

Zest of 1 lemon

1 cinnamon stick

5 cups water

⅔ cup rice flour

⅔ cup sugar

Put the ground almonds in a mixing bowl with the lemon zest and cinnamon stick. Bring the water to a boil and pour over the almonds and aromatics. Stir well, cover, and let set for 6 hours, stirring occasionally.

Remove the cinnamon stick and discard. Strain the almond mixture through a cheesecloth, reserving the liquid. Press out every last drop of the almond milk. Discard the solids.

Set out 4 flan dishes, dessert cups, or small, individual terra-cotta *cazuelas*.

Heat the reserved almond milk in a large saucepan over medium heat. Bring to a boil, and continue boiling for 2 minutes, then reduce the heat to low. Very gradually add the rice flour and then the sugar while stirring constantly. Cook, stirring constantly, for 10 minutes, until there are no lumps in the pudding and the taste is smooth and sweet. Remove from the heat and strain out any lumps, if necessary. Pour into the flan dishes. Let cool and then refrigerate for at least 1 hour to set.

Just before serving, toast the slivered almonds in a small dry skillet until golden and fragrant. Roughly chop them and sprinkle evenly over the individual puddings.

Sources

• • •

The Spanish Table

(206) 682-2827

www.spanishtable.com

The best all-around source for Spanish rice cookware, including paella pans, *cazuelas,* wood fire stands, gas-ring burners, and tripod mounts. They also carry Spanish rices, olive oils, *pimentón,* preserved snails, wines, and other products.

Sur la Table

(800) 243-0852

www.surlatable.com

A good cookware selection, including Le Creuset casseroles, and some Spanish specialty food items, such as olive oils and saffron.

Williams-Sonoma

(877) 812-6235

www.williams-sonoma.com

Another large, complete cookware store that also sells some specialty Spanish tools and foods.

La Tienda

(888) 472-1022

www.tienda.com

A good selection of paella supplies, including pans, burners, and stands, as well as *cazuelas* and imported Spanish foods including Bomba and Calasparra rice.

La Española Meats

(310) 539-0455

www.laespanolameats.com

This Los Angeles food importer sells plenty of Spanish foods, including a variety of imported rices and their own Spanish-style sausages. They also carry paella pans, *cazuelas,* fire stands, and gas burners.

PaellaPans.com

(845) 855-9518

www.paellapans.com

A great online source for paella pans, gas burners and leg supports, and wood fire stands.

Whole Foods Market

www.wholefoodsmarket.com

A national chain specializing in organic and natural products, this is an excellent source for fresh rabbit, duck, game, poussin, squab, and monkfish, as well as imported Spanish oils, olives, wines, and cheeses.

Trader Joe's

(800) 746-7857

www.traderjoes.com

An excellent specialty retail grocery chain with some imported Spanish goods.

WHERE TO BUY PAELLA PANS AND OTHER RICE-MAKING EQUIPMENT IN SPAIN

El Corte Inglés

(34) 902 22 44 11
www.elcorteingles.es
This large department store chain has branches in many Spanish cities. They are well stocked with kitchen equipment, and all of the rice essentials can be found in the grocery store on the bottom floor. Many branches have a Club del Gourmet, a small, highly selective shop that sells the finest food products, including saffron, oils, rices, and so on.

Ferretería Guillermo Pedrós

Vieja de la Paja
Palco exterior 1, 2, and 3
Valencia
(34) 96 391 7891
A well-stocked, decades-old stall along the outside of Valencia's Mercado Central that specializes in paella equipment.

Manuel Ortiz García

Palco exterior 8 y 10
Valencia
(34) 96 391 8666
Another well-stocked, well-established stall along the outside of Valencia's Mercado Central that specializes in paella equipment.

Antigua Hojalatería

Petxina, 8 (beside Las Ramblas)
Barcelona
(34) 93 317 7584
A small shop, but stuffed with cooking utensils. It is tucked away on a tiny street just south of La Boqueria market.

Targa

Plaza Palacio, 5 y 6
08003 Barcelona
(34) 93 319 9241
An old-fashioned, well-stocked, no-nonsense "hardware" store that caters to home cooks and restaurants.

WHERE TO EAT AUTHENTIC PAELLAS
AND OTHER RICE DISHES IN SPAIN

You will find paella served all over Spain, but restaurants that serve truly good, authentic paellas are a select group. The ones listed below (by geography, radiating south from Valencia, then skipping north to Barcelona) are some of the best. They include legendary places, such as Casa Salvador in Cullera (just south of Valencia), which has a kitchen with twenty-three flaming burners dedicated to paellas. Others are presided over by creative chefs, like Quique Dacosta at El Poblet in Dénia, south of Valencia. Ask for the rice specialty of the house. It's likely the waiter will say that everything is a specialty, in which case, put it another way: *¿Qué arroz servís más?* ("Which rice do you serve the most?") Order that one.

Casa Roberto
Maestro Gozalbo, 19
Valencia
(34) 96 395 1361

L'Estimat
Paseo Neptuno, 16
Valencia
(34) 96 371 1018
www.lestimat.com

La Pepica
Paseo Neptuno, 6
Valencia
(34) 96 371 0366
www.lapepica.com

La Riuà
Calle del Mar, 27
(parallel to Calle La Paz)
Valencia
(34) 96 391 4571

El Tossal
Quart, 6
Valencia
(34) 96 391 5913

Casa Carmina
Embarcadero, 4
El Saler (just south of Valencia
in the Albufera)
(34) 96 183 0254

L'Establiment
Camino del Estell
El Palmar (just south of
Valencia in the Albufera)
(34) 96 162 0100

Raco de L'Olla
Carretera de El Palmar, 21
El Palmar (just south of
Valencia in the Albufera)
(34) 96 162 0172

Casa Salvador
L'Estany de Cullera
Cullera (south of Valencia
just past the Albufera)
(34) 96 172 0136
www.casasalvador.com

Casa la Abuela
Reina, 17
Xàtiva (south of Valencia)
(93) 96 228 1085

El Poblet
Carretera Les Marines,
Kilometer 2.5
Dénia (south of Valencia)
(34) 96 578 4179
www.elpoblet.com

La Vinya del Senyor
Avenida Sarrià, 15
Barcelona
(34) 93 410 2511

L'Arrosseria Xàtiva
Bordeus, 35
Barcelona
(34) 93 322 6531
www.arrosseriaxativa.com

Julius
Passeig Joan Borbó, 66
Barcelona
(34) 93 224 7035
www.eljulius.com

7 Portes
Passeig d'Isabel II, 14
Barcelona
(34) 93 319 3033
www.7portes.com

Select Bibliography

• • •

Agulló, Ferran. *Llibre de la cuina catalana.* Barcelona: Lliberia Puig i Alfonso, 1933.

Alcover, Antoni M., and Francesc de B. Moll Casasnovas. *Diccionari català-valencià-balear,* 9th edition. Palma de Mallorca: Moll, 1983. www.dcvb.iecat.net

Alford, Jeffrey, and Naomi Duguid. *Seductions of Rice.* New York: Artisan, 1998.

An Anonymous Andalusian Cookbook of the 13th Century, translated by Charles Perry. www.daviddfriedman.com/Medieval/Cookbooks/Andalusian/andalusian_contents

Andrews, Colman. *Catalan Cuisine.* Boston: Harvard Common, 1988.

Bittman, Mark. *Fish: The Complete Guide to Buying and Cooking.* New York: Hungry Minds, 1994.

Davidson, Alan. *The Oxford Companion to Food.* Oxford: Oxford University Press, 1999.

———. *The Tio Pepe Guide to the Seafood of Spain and Portugal.* Málaga: Santana, 2002.

Fàbrega, Jaume. *Traditional Catalan Cooking,* translated by Paul Martin. Barcelona: La Magrana, 1997.

Hemphill, Ian. *Spice Notes.* Sydney, Australia: Macmillan, 2000.

Lladonosa i Giró, Josep. *El gran llibre de la cuina catalana.* Barcelona: Empúries, 1991.

———. *El llibre dels arrossos del 7 Portes i alters arrossos.* Barcelona: Empúries, 1999.

———. *El llibro de la cocina catalana.* Madrid: Alianza, 1988.

López, Domènec. *Las mejores recetas con arroz.* Barcelona: RBA Libros, 2003.

Luján, Néstor. *Como piñones mondados.* Barcelona: Folio, 1994.

———. *Diccionari Luján de gastronomia catalana.* Barcelona: La Campana, 1990.

March, Lourdes. *El libro de la paella y de los arroces.* Madrid: Alianza, 1985.

Millo, Lorenzo. *La gastronomía de la Comunidad Valenciana.* Valencia: Prensa Valenciana, 1992.

Petràs, Llorenç. *La millor cuina dels bolets.* Barcelona: Empúries, 2000.

Prádanos, Jorge, and Pedro Gómez Carrizo. *El gran diccionario de cocina.* Barcelona: RBA Libros, 2003.

Queralt Tomás, M. Carme. *La cuina de les Terres de l'Ebre.* Valls: Cossetània, 2000.

Riera, Ignasi. *Diccionari de la cuina catalana.* Barcelona: Edicions 62, 2002.

Tovar, Rosa. *Arroces.* Madrid: El País Aguilar, 2003.

Wright, Clifford A. *Mediterranean Vegetables.* Boston: Harvard Common, 2001.

Acknowledgments

* * *

Thanks for this book necessarily begin with my mother-in-law, Rosa, who served me my first paella, taught me to appreciate it, eventually how to make it, and then, in a step towards independence, gave me my first paella pan.

Thanks, too, to the rest of the Borràs family in Catalunya—especially my father-in-law, Tomàs, and sisters-in-law, Carmina, Rosa Maria, and Marien—and to my family in the U.S., especially my parents, Bill and Joanne Koehler.

In Barcelona, I am indebted to those in the markets and small shops who always offer a steady stream of advice, tips, and wisdom, including my fishmonger at Peixos Marina, the four ladies that front my butcher's, Carnisseria Marsol, Antoni Cot at Bouquet d'Aromes, and Llorenç Petràs at Petràs Fruits, as well as Albert Asín at Bar Pinotxo. *Moltes gràcies* to Ismael Prados for his generous thoughts and superlative *caldero* that I am pleased to include here. Also appreciative thanks to Montse Catalán (in Barcelona) and Montse Boschdemont (in Canet d'Adri).

In Sueca (Valencia), thanks to Santos Ruiz Álvarez, director of the Denominacíon de Origen Arroz de Valencia, and in Valencia, to Maria Luz Valero and Jesus Mansilla, and, in the Mercado Central, Pepa and Amparo at Caracoles Peribañez.

I would like to thank those who indirectly aided this book by supporting my writing and my cooking, namely Tod Nelson (who also read the book's introduction), Jim Finley, Kirk Giloth, and Robert Brown on the page, and Natalia Reixach, Jaume Pascual, Valeria Judkowski, Pascal Poignard, and Caspar in the kitchen and around the table. And Aaron Wehner and Teresa Barrenechea for their always illuminating and inspiring conversations, and Elizabeth Andoh for her long-distance support.

A very special thanks to Naomi Duguid and Jeffrey Alford who have generously offered their advice and support on matters of writing, food, life, kids, travel, and photography over the last years.

I am grateful to my various editors who have supported and sharpened my writing, including Jocelyn Zuckerman at *Gourmet*, Kate Heddings and Tina Ujlaki at *Food & Wine*, Katie Bacon at the *Atlantic Monthly*, Jeanne McManus at the *Washington Post*, Catharine Hamm and Craig Nakano at the *Los Angeles Times*, Jennifer Wolcott at the *Christian Science Monitor*, Allison Cleary and Patsy Jamieson at *Eating Well*, Michelle Wildgen at *Tin House*, Allison Arieff at *dwell*, Abigail Seymour and Cari Jackson, both formerly at U.S. Airway's *Attaché*, and the consistent Michael Buller at *Continental*.

Copious thanks, too, to my superlative agent, Doe Coover, whose enthusiasm never wavers.

On the book itself, I would like to thank Pep Blancafort for his work on the plated shots and Deborah Kops for her copyediting. At Chronicle Books, many thanks to the enthusiastic Leslie Jonath who initially recommended me for the project, and the team there who helped make this book what it is, including Doug Ogan, Tera Killip, Ben Shaykin, and Vanessa Dina. A very big thank you to my editor, Amy Treadwell, for her initial idea and continuous support in the project.

Lastly, love and appreciation to my young daughters, Alba and Maia, and my wife, Eva, my first reader and photo editor, who has taught me much and shared everything.

Index

• • •

Table of Equivalents

• • •

The exact equivalents in the following tables have been rounded for convenience.

LIQUID/DRY MEASURES

U.S.	METRIC
¼ teaspoon	1.25 milliliters
½ teaspoon	2.5 milliliters
1 teaspoon	5 milliliters
1 tablespoon (3 teaspoons)	15 milliliters
1 fluid ounce (2 tablespoons)	30 milliliters
¼ cup	60 milliliters
⅓ cup	80 milliliters
½ cup	120 milliliters
1 cup	240 milliliters
1 pint (2 cups)	480 milliliters
1 quart (4 cups, 32 ounces)	960 milliliters
1 gallon (4 quarts)	3.84 liters
1 ounce (by weight)	28 grams
1 pound	454 grams
2.2 pounds	1 kilogram

LENGTH

U.S.	METRIC
⅛ inch	3 millimeters
¼ inch	6 millimeters
½ inch	12 millimeters
1 inch	2.5 centimeters

OVEN TEMPERATURE

°F	°C	GAS
250	120	½
275	140	1
300	150	2
325	160	3
350	180	4
375	190	5
400	200	6
425	220	7
450	230	8
475	240	9
500	260	10